# YOU MAKE THE DIFFERENCE

## THROUGH
# ENJOYABLE & VALUABLE VOLUNTEERING

Kay Kay

In collaboration with Tim Kay

You Make the Difference
www.youmakethedifference.net

Second Edition
First Edition published in 2012

Book designed and published by Tim Kay
University of Life

www.unioflife.net

# DEDICATION

This book is dedicated to the wonderful people with whom it has been my privilege and pleasure to share my volunteering experiences and to the many more who commit time and effort through their volunteering to make a positive difference in our world.

# CONTENTS

# ACKNOWLEDGMENTS

I am grateful to Tim Kay for his creative and supportive approach to publishing this book. To Jane Cotton for her eagle eye and for the wealth of knowledge and experience of working in the Voluntary and Community Sector that she brings to editing the books in this series.

I deeply appreciate all of those wonderful volunteers who I have been privileged to work alongside in so many situations and projects around the world. Whether these have been easy or challenging, simple or complex, enjoyable or hazardous, your willingness and dedication has been inspirational!

The saying, 'Money makes the world go round', is not accurate in my world. In my experience, it is Love that makes the world go round! It is many of the words that come under the heading of Love, which describe the attitudes and the actions of all of those people who are committed to making the difference through their volunteering.

# 1

# WHY VOLUNTEER?

Why volunteer? Why bother to do something that is of benefit to others that has seemingly no benefit for us as individuals? Why engage in activities that might be challenging or less than comfortable when we could be relaxing and taking things easy? Why spend precious time in being of service to others when we could use it for making more money or in finding nice ways for spending what we have? Why be involved in projects created to improve health and wellbeing of people we do not know or to increase environmental, social and community sustainability when we could be engaging in some of the many enjoyable leisure pursuits available to us?

## What's the point?

When faced with many personal difficulties or when contemplating a world full of seemingly insurmountable problems, there is a tendency among some of us to raise our hands in despair and groan, 'what's the point?' or even 'there is nothing any of us can do about these circumstances!' Sometimes a situation seems so overwhelming that we might feel too daunted to even contemplate making a difference to it. This is understandable, and yet, how does this help?

On the other hand, some of us have very little awareness of the huge difficulties that many other people have to deal with every day. And that not only do these difficulties exist in far-flung places around the world they also exist in our local communities. My experience, research and observation of some of the causes of and the reasons for an expanding need for volunteers are described in the postscript at the end of the book.

# Inaction is rarely a solution!

*There is a story about the man who noticed that the whole length of the beach he was walking along was littered with starfish, washed up by the overnight storm. The high tide had left thousands of them stranded as the water began to recede.*

*He watched a boy picking up starfish and putting them in deeper water so the tide would take them back out to sea. The man laughed and said to the boy 'what difference do you think that's going to make? There are thousands of them!'*

*The boy stared at him for a moment and then, gently picking up another starfish, replied, 'it will make a difference to this one.'*

*The man paused for a moment, then took off his shoes and socks, rolled up his trousers and started picking up starfish and placing them back in the water. As other people came on to the beach, they joined in the rescue.*

I like this story because it contains so many useful messages:
1. It only takes one person to make a difference.
2. Helping is better than not helping.
3. When faced with a seemingly insurmountable problem, do whatever you can to alleviate it.
4. It is better to help than to scoff at the efforts of others.
5. Anyone can start a useful trend.
6. When you see someone doing something beneficial, regardless of the odds, join them.

It is worth remembering that there is always something that can be done about any situation. There is always a small change or improvement that can be made to make some positive difference to any circumstances.

### Choosing to volunteer

For most of us the reason for choosing to volunteer is that we care and want to help. We want to do something useful; we want to improve situations that are not working very well; we want to be part of the world's solutions rather than be part of the problems, we want to be involved in creating a better future; we want to make a difference.

> The notion that volunteers are 'do-gooders' or bountiful ladies dispensing charity is a thing of the past. Volunteers come in all shapes, sizes, ages, colors and genders and from every imaginable background.

Volunteering is becoming an important aspect of many people's lives. Many of us are always ready to assist our friends and neighbors who occasionally need a helping hand and we are quick to step forward when help is required after some local catastrophe such as fire or flood. We might not think of this as volunteering; instead, we consider it to be just helping out.

Some people volunteer because they observe a need that they could help with or they identify a useful role that they could fill. Often, people are moved to volunteer for emotional reasons. Their hearts are stirred by compassion for others or a desire to help improve situations and circumstances. Many people want to contribute some of their time and talents in their local community or to national or international programs of aid and support. There are those for whom volunteering is a source of interest or an opportunity for spending time with other people. For others, volunteering can be a stepping-stone towards employment.

> Volunteering can be simple, effective, rewarding, immensely valuable and very enjoyable.

# A lifetime of enjoyable volunteering

Volunteering has been a strong thread running through my life. In sharing my volunteering experiences with you I hope to show the variety of opportunities that have been available to one person; the mutual needs that have been met and the interest and the benefits that have been exchanged as a result of volunteering.

### My earliest recollection of volunteering

This was when, as a little girl, I helped an elderly neighbor, who was recovering from an illness, to pick and preserve the fruit from her garden. I did not know at the time that this could be considered to be volunteering because in those days many of the things that now fit under that heading were simply called 'helping out'.

Mrs. Thompson and I enjoyed some very companionable afternoons together that summer, although, I am not sure how much help she actually received from me. She seemed to find pleasure in a little girl's chatter and I learned from her there were other perspectives on the world than those of my family and school friends. I had not expected any of the jars of jam that she gave me at the end of our time together and I'm sure they tasted more delicious because I had not expected them.

## Duke of Edinburgh Award Scheme

It was through this scheme, in which I participated as a teenager, that I began to understand the value of volunteering. An important component of the scheme is that of being of service to others. It was through those acts of volunteer service that I learnt how interesting and rewarding volunteering could be.

I still remember the Saturday afternoons when I volunteered to be a non-deaf 'conversation partner' to be practiced upon by eager teenagers in a residential school for deaf children. During the time I spent with my deaf friends I learned how essential it is to give them my full attention and to be completely present with the person who was speaking to me. Noticing the difference this approach made when also speaking with people who could hear had a profound effect on my listening behavior. This has influenced my work in Constructive Communication.

## Different ways

Sometimes my volunteered actions have been simple, easily offered methods of support, such as babysitting to allow financially stretched young parents to have an evening out together. At other times, activities have involved some effort, as when inviting a little girl to spend a few weeks with me and my young family, as part of a scheme to offer deprived inner-city children a holiday staying with families who lived in the countryside. I learned a lot from little Agnes during those weeks, and although we lost touch, I often think of her.

## Based upon needs

Many of my volunteer activities have been based upon some need that I had.

It was to provide some care for my children that I first became part of a group setting up a crèche, then helping out with a playgroup and later joining a parent teacher association. It has been my desire to learn from wise people and my wish to help others to do so that has led me to help with organizing conferences and arranging events to host inspirational speakers.

## Based upon experiences

Sometimes it has been the good experiences that have been catalysts for my volunteering. It was the help that I received as a young teenager to channel my wayward energies that led me in later life to initiate youth projects. (It also influenced my writing regarding listening to children). Some of my more difficult life experiences have also influenced my desire to help others experiencing similar circumstances. It was my early experiences of being without a secure home that persuaded me later to be a supporter of the work of SHELTER. Having a rare blood type resulted in my volunteering in the Canadian Red Cross blood transfusion service.

## Based upon interest and passion

Interest in and passion for subjects has frequently led me towards some supportive action. It was through my passion for the performing and visual arts that I became involved in activities to raise the money to build an exciting new Theatre in my city and to participate in the planning of the city's Arts Festival.

## Short and long

At times, my voluntary commitment has been for a short time, as when caring for the cat of a neighbor who was in hospital. At other times my volunteering has required a long-term commitment such as the creation and management of several networks. One of these was the international support network, Friends of Findhorn, which I started in 1990 and which took three and a half years of part time volunteering from me until it became established firmly enough for the Findhorn Foundation to integrate it as one of their departments.

With the growth of the Internet this has since evolved into the Internet-based Global Network, which is still going strong and has thousands of members. I had no intention of travelling when I created Friends of Findhorn. And yet for years afterwards this network of wonderful people offered me supportive contacts in many countries around the World.

## Simple tasks

Sometimes, simple, practical tasks have produced some delightful results. I experienced this when I regularly used my skills of hairdressing to cut the hair of children in a local care home. It was heart-warming to see the blossoming of these children's self-esteem as a result of receiving an individual hairstyle designed to make the most of their features and the quality of their hair. These youngsters also seemed to benefit from having the opportunity to talk to a person, not immediately involved in their lives, who gave them some undivided attention.

## Things just need to be done

There have been times when things have just had to be done, when there was a need to muck-in and do whatever was necessary, such as supporting neighbors, friends and strangers in dealing with local difficulties or helping with the clean-up after some calamity.

### Surprising rewards...

I have found that the rewards of volunteering come in surprising ways. I have happily voluntarily convened meetings and facilitated discussions and mediations to resolve local community conflict, to offer coaching and mentoring to individuals and community organizations, and to run workshops and training programs in subjects that were believed would be of assistance to community development. Occasionally this resulted in future paid work, sometimes from unexpected quarters.

### ...And support

It seems that not only rewards come from unexpected sources; so does support. On my travels in the mid and late 1990s, when I was in my 50s, I discovered that many local people in the developing world and newly emerging nations were gallantly attempting to initiate projects and to support actions for the benefit of the people in their communities. It was clear that they only required a little training in a number of simple skills and some coaching and mentoring in order to be extremely effective.

These courageous people had little or no money and it took ridiculous amounts of time and effort to acquire funding for this type of work, even to cover expenses. So I worked pro-bono and used my own resources to cover my expenses. I was happy to receive accommodation, food and some transportation in exchange for my work.

Just as my resources were running out, a generous friend stepped in to help. He made me a signatory on his gold AMEX credit card account!

It was this and other types of support, that freed me to spend a number of years wandering the planet voluntarily offering my skills and experience to the people who asked for them and whose work I wanted to assist. Very occasionally people would find a little money to offer me, which helped with travel expenses and with the replacement of the occasional necessary item.

Surprisingly, during this time, I rarely needed to use the Gold Card. Just knowing that it was there for emergencies seemed to be enough to keep me trusting the Universal flow of giving and receiving.

### A fabulous way of working

I discovered that this was a fabulous way of working. I was privileged to be alongside remarkable people who were making a significant difference in their parts of the world. I was unencumbered by red tape, the need to find funding or any other kind of restriction. During this time I learned so much about other cultures and the indomitable nature of the human spirit.

During these years I usually stayed in the homes of the people I worked with or with their family members, colleague's, friends or neighbors. These homes were in cities, towns and villages and spanned anything from the guest wing in the home of a millionaire, to a thatched, mud hut. A great many were apartments in utilitarian, high-rise apartment blocks in countries that were once part of the USSR. Modes of transport were equally diverse and included a camel and a Presidential jet!

Regardless of whether they were in Novosibirsk in Siberia, or the cloud forest in Central America or anywhere in between, people showed their appreciation of my efforts by their eagerness to learn, their willingness to participate, and their huge commitment to using the information and their newly acquired or improved skills for the benefit of their communities.

It has been a privilege to witness the commitment of those who have taken on projects and initiatives and the courage of people who have stepped forward to continue with social improvement in some extremely challenging circumstances.

## Near and far

This has not only happened in exotic or far-flung places. Such wonderfully courageous and committed people emerged from a meeting convened in Scotland by a group of us in our town to discuss a worrying situation regarding local teenagers and the town's future. This meeting led to the formation of a steering group to organize a three-day Future Search event to resolve these concerns.

Everyone engaged in this event volunteered his or her time. Some handled administration and logistics before, during and after the event. Others ran the crèche, handled the catering (most of the food was donated by local food production companies and bakeries) or provided transportation.

Many people were involved in fundraising to pay for the hire of the hall and other essential expenses. Each person who represented one of the many stakeholder groups in the community: parents, teachers, young people, youth leaders, social workers, business leaders, police and Church leaders, either volunteered their time, persuaded their employers to give them leave of absence or to send them to the event as representatives.

The facilitators of this event were professionals who were trained and accredited to facilitate the Future Search process. Collectively they donated dozens of hours of facilitation time to the event. They asked only that their expenses be covered.

The results of this event were astounding and still relevant almost 20 years later!

This is an example of how the one small act of creating an opportunity for people to gather together in a way that encourages communication, creativity and commitment can have a profound effect on the future of a neighborhood a community, a town, and on everyone involved.

## Benefitting from Technology

This is now providing so many new and easy ways for being of service to others: searching online for organizations and projects in which to become involved; being instantly informed of events through which to be of help; being in immediate contact with inspiring people and projects, and offering and receiving regular encouragement.

Now that I am sharing, through my writing, ideas, information and the skills I have acquired, this technology makes it possible for me to work with my editor in Scotland and my publisher and web master in Sweden. This technology allows me to continue to volunteer my time through offering information, insights and experience in handy Guides that can be downloaded for FREE from my website by anyone who might find them interesting and useful.

## Added value

To sum up my experience of volunteering I would say that it has offered me so many possibilities for becoming a small part of the solution and making a positive contribution to the world around me. Volunteering has added a valuable extra dimension to the person I am, it has made a significant improvement to the quality of my life, it has often been very enjoyable and, it has made me happy!

I encourage everyone to join in!

# 2

# MAKING THE DIFFERENCE THROUGH VOLUNTEERING

*'The world is going to hell in a handcart! I want to make a difference to that, yet I don't know what I can do. I feel helpless and hopeless!'*

*Helen said this several years ago when she came to me for some Personal Culture consultation regarding her feelings of despair about the world and her sense of disempowerment to do anything to improve it.*

*Over a few sessions, she identified and explored the options for the many ways, small and large, in which she could make a positive difference to the world around her. She discovered that every option she chose, that had positive benefits for others, also resulted in positive benefits to her own life – and vice versa.*

*Helen's enthusiasm for making a difference became contagious, inspiring other people to bring about changes in their personal circumstances and to make a meaningful contribution to the community in which they lived.*

My observation is that every one of us makes a difference to the world around us moment by moment, all day long. We do so with our thoughts, our words and our deeds. Sometimes we are conscious of what we're thinking, saying and doing and other times we are not. It is usually when we are unaware of the effect that we have on the world around us that we become part of the problem. By waking up to this we each can choose to become part of the solution.

*As she was creating her strategies for making a difference, Helen asked me how it was that I could always stay so positive? My answer to her was that I believe that being positive is a choice, just as being negative is. Every moment of every day presents each of us with opportunities to make either a positive or a negative difference to our lives and to the lives of others. The trick to being an effective and smart human being is to chose to make a positive difference!'*

The choice to become part of the solution in any situation may require a change of mind or a change of heart. It might require action and involvement over a period of time. Or it might just mean giving someone an encouraging word or a smile.

It seems obvious to me that it is the waking up of each one of us to our place in the world and to the potential for our personal and collective evolution that will make the difference to the future.

# Waking up to reality

By waking up to reality we become more aware of the circumstances that could benefit from being changed or improved. By identifying the reality of any situation we can begin to recognize what beneficial improvements could be made. By understanding the reality of attitudes and behaviors that create problems we can begin making beneficial changes to those. By realistically exploring appropriate options we can identify strategies to achieve appropriate outcomes.

### What's the difference?

The difference you can make is between being part of the problem or part of the solution. That is a matter of choice. Your choice!

There are three options to this:

**1.** Be aware when any of your attitudes, thoughts, words, actions and behavior might contribute to the problems in your life and in the world around you.

**2.** Identify your attitudes, thoughts, words, actions or behavior that could bring about solutions and improvements in your life and in the world around you.

**3.** Choose those in 2. Simple!

> Making this choice may take a little more thought, patience and effort than the old knee-jerk or unconscious choices that created problems or did nothing to solve them. However, the difference that these choices make can be life and world changing.

## Working with the choices

In order to make a difference, some people chose to concentrate their efforts on developing themselves, their relationships or their children. Others focus upon enhancing or improving their workplace or their profession. Many become engaged in some aspect of society, of the environment or the many humanitarian endeavors that are in need of support.

There are people who prefer to make individual efforts. There are others who join with groups and organizations to bring about the changes they wish to see. Where these do not exist, some people have the tenacity to create projects, to attract the necessary support and to gather around them people willing to help in achieving objectives.

By waking up to what is really going on and by making conscious choices about it, people not only make a difference, they motivate others to do the same.

It is worth remembering that it is through changing our thinking, attitudes and behavior and by demonstrating useful and effective actions that we can all make an enormous, positive difference to the society in which we live.

## What are your options?

There are many ways in which you could make a difference to the lives of those around you. These might be:

a. Being alert and aware of the reality of situations.
b. Pausing to think before speaking or acting.
c. Making moment-by-moment positive choices.
d. Seeking constructive, workable options and creative solutions to difficult situations.
e. Looking for ways to help rather than hinder.
f. Using your time and talents to benefit others.
g. Working cooperatively with others.
h. Creating opportunities for improvement.
i. Being positive, encouraging and supportive in the face of adversity and encouraging others to do the same.

# Who, me?

'It is only special people who make a difference in the world'. 'Nothing can be done by ordinary people'. 'What could I possibly do that would make any difference?' and 'who me?' are the sorts of statements I have heard from people over the years.

Experience indicates that these sentiments are based on either lack of self-belief or an expectation that someone else is responsible for solving problems.

## Ordinary people

What is an ordinary person? I cannot remember meeting any! I have met many people who struggle daily against all sorts of odds to make life work for themselves and those around them. They do not make a fuss or think the ways in which they cope is out of the ordinary.

I know people whose approach to life and everyday work could be hailed as heroic, and yet they do not think of themselves as special. I have met many whose attitudes and way of being with the people they meet makes a positive difference to those people. I know of many others who regularly contribute their time and resources to help those around them or people they have never met.

None of these people would consider themselves to be extraordinary. So what makes a person ordinary?

> Perhaps ordinary describes us when we are hiding our uniqueness and our true selves, when we believe we are less than we are, when we do not yet recognize our full potential or the difference we make in the world.

If, when considering whether or not you could make a difference to any situation, your response is 'who, me?' my question would be 'if not you, then who?'

# Changing our minds

Some of us seem unable or unwilling to take responsibility for the actions needed to bring about changes. We may doubt our abilities to alter conditions, influence outcomes or create the results we wish for. Our life history may have become distilled into a victim consciousness so strong that although we feel everything deeply, we behave as spectators of life; seemingly helpless to effect circumstance.

It is not unusual for people to seek coaching in the expectation of being told what to do. Some people are dismayed even angry to discover that a coach's role is to help them to discover their own solutions to their difficulties or to find their own ways of making improvements in their lives. It seems difficult for some people to accept that deep down they already know most of the options available to them and the wisest course of action for them to take.

In my experience, people just need a little help in recognizing these, and some support in creating workable strategies.

> If you are wondering who can really make a difference to the challenges in your life and in your world, I suggest that it would be you! When that difference is in regard to your thoughts and attitudes, surely, it can only be you!

## Who is responsible?

When it comes to wanting things to improve or changes to happen in the world, many people seem to take the view that the responsibility lies elsewhere.

This 'elsewhere' appears to be populated by people called 'they'. There is often an assumption that 'they' will: 'spot the problem', 'do something about the situation' or 'sort something out'. This might not be an unreasonable assumption when 'they' are paid to do those things.

However, what about the occasions when something needs to happen that is not part of a job? When some situation needs attention or a problem needs solving and there is no apparent person to take care of it? That is when we might cast around within the vague mass of 'they' for individuals to take responsibility. These individuals are usually called 'somebody's'.

We might anticipate, imagine or hope that 'somebody' will notice there is a problem. That 'somebody' will do something, report it, clean up the mess, call a meeting, gather support for... start a project to...' If this doesn't happen we might express our amazement. 'You would think somebody would... Surely somebody could...?'

If we are disappointed or outraged we might proclaim 'somebody really should... why hasn't somebody...? It's disgraceful that somebody hasn't...!'

Of course, there are people who take it upon themselves to make a positive difference, even when they don't have to, when it's not their job or when nobody else will. These people are often called 'those'. 'Those' are the people who raise awareness, provide help and support, start discussions, call meetings, create projects, etc. that make a positive difference in society.

'Those' are probably people we admire. We appreciate the efforts and applaud the achievements of 'those' people. 'Those' people may inspire us so much that we might offer them some financial contribution or other forms of support. 'Those' people provide us with opportunities to feel good about ourselves as we make some contribution. By inspiring us to become involved, even if only in a small way, 'those' people help us to take our first steps towards making a difference.

**Changing words**

One of these first steps could be stopping using the words 'they', 'somebody' and 'those' people and replacing them with the word 'we'. This tiny change of language can bring about an enormous change in attitude. Shifting the responsibility for anything from 'they' to 'we' acknowledges the fundamental condition on this planet of, 'we are all in this together'. The recognition of this has probably done more to make a difference to improving situations than any other statement.

In most circumstances 'we' can do what is required to make the desired difference. In the democratic world 'we' elect our governments, we influence the way our society is managed and we have many of the world's resources at our disposal.

> Remember, with a 'yes we can' attitude, we can sway opinion, start trends, influence business decisions and elect reforming presidents and influence improvements and beneficial changes to laws.

The next and vital step to be taken by anyone intent on making a personal difference in the world is the shift from saying 'we' to 'me'.

Here is a handy hint. Suppose for a moment that you are pointing your finger (real or metaphorical) out 'there' in search of a 'somebody' to make a difference to some situation. If you take a look at your hand you will notice that one finger will be pointing forwards and outwards, while the other three fingers on your hand are pointing backwards and inwards - towards you. Perhaps that is a hint to indicate who could step up to do something – you!

**Could and might**

You and I are unlikely to go very far together if your attitude to all this is

'Well, I could' or 'I might'. I regard these as weak and wishy-washy statements, lacking in substance and commitment. 'I could' and 'I might' rarely achieve anything except lost opportunities, disappointment, disempowerment, frustration and guilt. Along with, 'I'll try', I recommend these statements be erased from your vocabulary.

None of the people I know who are making a positive difference in the world use these words. They say 'I can!' 'I will!' and use phrases such as 'Let's do it!' 'We can do it!' and 'What will it take to achieve this?'

> Regarding guilt. From my experiences I have learned that guilt is a useless, damaging, negative emotion. Any guilty feelings you have, resulting from what you could or might have done in the past, are unlikely to make a positive contribution to any situation.

A useful method for dealing successfully with feelings of guilt is to: learn what you can from the experience; forgive yourself; apologize, if appropriate, and move on to doing something more positive.

### The questions

I have learned that there are very few circumstances that cannot be improved upon in an individual's life, in the lives of other people, in society and in the world.

My questions to you are:
1.  Where do you see need for improvement?
2.  How can you help?
3.  If not now, when?

I have asked these questions of many people. The stories I have heard about voluntary activities, of projects and of the work of community groups have been inspirational. They became the motivation for this and the other books in the series – You Make The Difference.

## Good reasons for volunteering

There are many good reasons for volunteering, however, most people volunteer for reasons that would fit the following main categories:

### Caring

They are caring people who want to help.

Some people create projects or become volunteers in organizations when they, or the people they care about, need whatever it is that is being provided. People volunteer in projects and organizations that have helped them, or someone close to them, in the past. Some organizations have a reputation for care that inspires volunteers to join them:

*"The capacity to care is what gives life its deepest significance." Pablo Casals.*

## Using skills

They are looking for ways to use their skills for the benefit of others. These are the people who can see that their talents could be useful to individuals or organizations. They feel their skills could be more beneficially employed than they are in their present circumstances. People might choose to volunteer in a project, a group or an organization where their skills and experience would be most effective.

## Interest and passions

They want to do something worthwhile in the areas of their interests and passions.

## Self-improvement

Some people want to learn new skills, build or gain experience or rebuild their confidence. They realize that some aspect of their present circumstances might be improved by opportunities offered through volunteering.

## Making contact

Some volunteers are seeking respite from isolation by making contact with others for companionship or friendship.

## Using time

Those with a lot of time on their hands may want to do something interesting or useful with that time. People such as retired or unemployed people or young people during a gap year or the summer holidays, and people who have no need to earn a living

## Travel

Some volunteer work offers opportunity for people to travel abroad and work in countries and cultures quite different from their own.

## Fulfillment

People often volunteer to create more meaning and purpose in their lives.

**Happiness**

Research is now proving what many of us already know – being helpful makes us happy! It appears that the chemicals released into our body as a result of being kind and helpful produce strong feelings of wellbeing. This research indicates that being of help to others could bring us more lasting happiness than many other things, including making more money or acquiring more stuff.

> Many people volunteer for a combination of these reasons. It seems to me that all of these reasons are valid and none of them are better than any other. Those who need and benefit from the volunteers input rarely mind what people's reasons are for volunteering.

# The benefits of volunteering

In my experience, there are many benefits to be gained from volunteering. People have told me that they receive so much through their volunteering and that their lives are so enriched by it that they are amazed that they did not volunteer sooner; and cannot imagine not being engaged in some voluntary activity or other during the rest of their lives.

These are some of the benefits you could enjoy through volunteering:
1.  You could meet new people and form new friendships.
2.  You could pursue new or old interests and passions.
3.  You could offer care, help and support to those less fortunate than yourself.
4.  You could show your gratitude and make your contribution through volunteering to organizations that have been supportive to you or those you care about.
5.  You could learn new skills or find new uses for your current skills and abilities.
6.  You could discover ways of using your time more effectively.
7.  There could be opportunities to gain work experience and find ways of adapting to new circumstances.
8.  You could travel abroad and work in situations very different from those you would find at home.
9.  Opportunities for paid work could become available to you

through your volunteering experience and the contacts you make.

10. You could develop yourself as a person and improve your self-confidence.
11. You could increase the way in which you value yourself as you see how others value you.
12. You could have an increased sense of purpose and gain fulfillment from making a positive contribution to the world in which you live.

## Making contacts

Aside from the emotional satisfaction that you could receive, volunteering might help to open up new channels in your life. Many of us can slip into a routine that could close us off from new opportunities. Volunteering can bring us back into contact with the largest community of all, humanity.

In business and corporate life there are many tried and trusted ways of advancement that take place outside of office hours: on the golf course or other sporting and social activities for example. Not all of us are interested in these activities and some of them may not be available to us for a number of reasons.

> Sometimes the reason is simply that in many situations women are often still not considered to be a part of the social fabric of business or corporate life.

## Women's networks

However, women have their own networks through which to get to know and to be mutually supportive of one another. These often entail volunteering. In some large companies this could be high-profile volunteer work. You might consider using your networking skills to make connections in the volunteer sector and to meet people with whom you might do business at some future date. Through volunteering together you will get to know something about one another's skills and accomplishments and so doors might gracefully open up.

## Giving and receiving

In my experience, volunteering can be at its most enjoyable and effective when offered in the spirit of giving and receiving.

Remember when considering volunteering, it is not unreasonable to wonder 'What's in it for me?' Finding a balance between giving and receiving might allow you to offer more of your time and skills. This has been shown to be an effective way to prevent burnout and resentment.

## Rewards

It seems that most of us find the greatest reward for volunteering to be the sense of satisfaction gained from knowing that something we have done has been helpful or has resulted in the world being a slightly better place. There are few things more satisfying than recognizing that a small effort on your part has made a positive difference and in knowing that your unique contribution has become part of the solution to some problem.

> It does seem to me that what goes around comes around. I have noticed there are often unexpected returns from deeds done with a good heart.

# What might get in the way of volunteering?

The reasons given for an inability or unwillingness to volunteer are usually practical ones. The solutions to these limitations will usually also be practical ones.

**Reason 1.** Some people feel that they don't have anything useful to contribute.
**Solution.** If you feel this way then there are processes in the next few chapters through which you can explore what you could offer.

**Reason 2.** Many people who would like to be of help to others consider that they have not enough or indeed any spare time for volunteering.
**Solution.** If this is your concern, then some of the ways suggested later might help you to reconsider how you currently use your time.

**Reason 3.** There are those who are reluctant to start volunteering because they believe that this would require a long-term commitment from them.
**Solution.** If this is your concern then be assured that this is not the case. There are plenty of opportunities for brief volunteering. You might choose to volunteer in occasional activities or at events that interest you. It could be useful for an organization to know that you could be called upon from time to time.

**Reason 4.** Even people who are keen to volunteer may not know how to go about it.
**Solution.** If you are unsure about the opportunities available for

volunteering you might find some useful pointers in the chapter on Finding your Niche.

**Reason 5.** Some people are reluctant to consider volunteering because they don't feel they would be comfortable around the sorts of people who they imagine would volunteer their time.
**Solution.** If this is how you feel then it might be helpful for you to know that there is not one type of person who volunteers. Every kind of person you can imagine, and probably several you cannot, occasionally or regularly volunteer their time and talents to support projects and causes that are meaningful to them.

**Reason 6.** There are people who do not consider volunteering because they believe that in order to do so they will have to become part of a group or an organization and they don't consider themselves to be 'joiners'.
**Solution.** If you feel this way then it would be useful to consider the many ways in which you could be of help on your own and in your personal and individual manner. Perhaps you could initiate a project to manage alone?

**Reason 7.** Some people might hold back from offering help and support to causes that tug at their heartstrings because they 'couldn't bear to see the suffering'.
**Solution.** If this applies to you then it could be supportive for you to remember that there are many ways in which you might be of tremendous help without coming face-to-face with those experiencing misfortune. Fundraising, campaigning, IT support and all the other aspects of administration could offer opportunities for you to help and support those you care about without being directly in contact with distressing situations.

**Reason 8.** There are those who have to cope with so many challenges in their own lives that they feel unable to consider helping other people.
**Solution.** If you feel this way about your own life then you may be comforted to learn how many people find release from their own troubles during the times that they are being of help to others. A self-empowering way of dealing with unhappiness or depression is to reach out to offer help to other people who are experiencing difficulties.

**Reason 9.** It is sometimes people's attitudes to the reasons behind problems that prevent them from attempting to make a difference through volunteering. Over the years I have heard these attitudes expressed in such statements as 'these people only have themselves to blame', 'it's their Karma', 'it's not up to me', 'God helps those who help themselves', 'why should I bother/put myself out/get involved?', 'What has anyone ever done for me?', 'I don't believe in doing something for nothing'.

Such statements as these often indicate feelings of separation by the people who make them from the people about whom these statements are made.

**Solution.** If you have found yourself saying or even thinking any of these things you might gain great benefit from making a small shift in your attitude. It is my experience that the following thoughts can help with that shift:

a. People often find themselves in difficult situations through no fault of their own.

b. Bad things happen to good people.

c. If your belief is that the situations in which people find themselves is due to their Karma, it is worth considering that your willingness to help them might provide you with brownie points toward your own Karma.

d. If you believe that God helps those who help themselves; could you be God's instrument in this?

e. Simply by adding one word to 'why should I?' To become: 'why should I not... put myself out/get involved/bother?' could bring about a profound change in your own life.

f. The grief or anger that is behind the question 'what has anyone ever done for me?' may be very deep. This can turn a person who has been hurt by the indifference of some people into a person who is indifferent to the suffering of others. If you feel that there was no one who 'did anything for you' when you needed them to, you might be able to ease your pain by being the one who now does what is needed by others.

g. The person you are is defined and demonstrated by the choices you make. Choosing to do something for nothing, choosing to be helpful just because you can, rather than just for what you can get out of it, is a clear demonstration of high human values.

---

Many of the concerns you have that may currently prevent you from becoming a volunteer might be easily overcome by a small shift in attitude. On the other hand, the very act of volunteering could help you to overcome some of these concerns.

---

# 3

# WHAT VOLUNTEERING COULD YOU DO?

**Q**

If you were certain that your volunteering would make a difference, what would you do?

## What inspires or concerns you?

Many of us are motivated to volunteer our time to an issue about which we have concerns or something that inspires us. Our concerns might develop in several ways:

1. Personal experience.
2. The recognition of a serious situation.
3. An understanding of the need for something to change.

You may already have something that concerns you deeply enough to galvanize you into action.

On the other hand, you may be wishing to make a difference and are not sure what it is that you want to make that difference.

## Course for concern

There are countless situations in our world that are cause for concern. Paying attention to what's happening around you and some simple researching locally or on the Internet could reveal some issue that would inspire you into volunteering.

Although concerns can vary enormously, they will usually fit under these broad headings:

➢ People
➢ Animals
➢ The environment
➢ Community
➢ Politics
➢ Religion/spirituality
➢ Historical or natural conservation
➢ The Arts
➢ Cultural preservation

Sometimes a concern about an issue is raised through changes to our own circumstances.

### *Robert*

*Robert was a senior corporate executive who thought very little about the environment until after the birth of his first grandchild. From then onwards it seemed that every time he turned on the TV, read his newspaper or went online, he was faced with some worrying environmental issue or other.*

*The more his interest became aroused, the more research he did. The more he learned, the more concerned he became about the kind of world that his little granddaughter would inherit.*

*Although he did not have a lot of time to spare he offered his services to an environmental campaign organization. He now chairs some of their strategy meetings and negotiations.*

---

Considering the issues that concern you or about which you have a deep interest or passion is a good place to start thinking about volunteering.

---

# What do you have to offer?

You might know exactly what kind of volunteering you want to do and what you want to offer. You perhaps already know the group or organization to which you wish to offer your time. Or you may not be clear about either of these. You might not be sure what you have to contribute or how the talents that you have could be of use to others.

These next few chapters are intended to assist you in identifying what you would like to achieve through volunteering; what mutual needs might be met through your volunteering; what you could offer; how you want to volunteer in what ways and when.

Each of the stages is designed to help you define and clarify the thoughts you already have on the subject, identify new and interesting options and develop strategies for making the most of your skills, interests, experience and time.

# Coaching yourself

You will get the most out of these next few chapters by treating them as a series of coaching sessions and taking time to explore the questions in each section. You can either make notes as you go along as indicated in the book or you might prefer to set up for yourself the conditions you would find when working one on one with a coach. In the latter case, follow the suggestions below for creating the ideal coaching conditions.

You might prefer to work with both of these options and find it useful to work through each chapter noting down your first thoughts on each topic in order to see some immediate results from the process. After this, you could then create your coaching environment and spend more time carefully considering each topic.

### Create the ideal coaching environment
A session with a coach usually lasts around an hour. During which time you would be sitting in a comfortable chair in calm surroundings. You would have a notebook or writing paper, pens and a perhaps a colored highlighter at your fingertips.

There would be no interruptions from other people or the telephone.

You may not find this easy to create for yourself if you are in the company of other people, with children demanding attention and the TV or sound system blaring away. You may need to be creative in finding space and time where you will not be interrupted.

At the beginning of each 'session' it would be wise to turn off your mobile phone and switch the landline on to the answering system. You might prefer to exchange the paper and pens for a computer if that is your preferred way of working.

# The valuable volunteer self-coaching program

## Overview

There are a number of steps to this self-coaching program:

**Step one.**
Identifying your two overall goals
**Step two.**
Exploring all that you have to offer
**Step three**
Identifying your preferred ways of being and working
**Step four**
Considering your time
**Step five**
Identifying your needs
**Step six**
Combining these to identify your unique combination
**Step seven**
Finding your perfect volunteering niche

> Each of these steps will be accompanied by the opportunity to look at your current reality regarding them and to identify and overcome any obstacles that could get in the way of you achieving your intended goals.

## Timing yourself

How much time you take over each of the steps is up to you. You might zip through some steps because the answers are clear to you. Other steps may take a while to explore. Regarding this, there are three things to be aware of:

1. If you take too long (meaning weeks) over the whole process you may lose momentum, especially if there are long gaps between sessions.
2. If you rush through the steps without giving careful consideration to your options you are likely to limit your possibilities.
3. This could be a great opportunity for you to recognize what a remarkable person you are and what a difference you already make to the world, just by being you.

# What are your goals?

In its essence, coaching is a supportive method for achieving goals. Some goals are specific: passing examinations, getting jobs or promotion, losing weight. Some are more encompassing: improving health or lifestyle; managerial approaches or relationship potential. A goal is having something to move towards like a distant light in the darkness.

Although there may be several aspects to the goals you wish to achieve through your volunteering, there are two main objectives:

**A.** What you want to achieve through your volunteering?

**B.** What you want to receive from your volunteering?

You may already know the answer to both of these questions in some detail. If not, your answers may lie among the categories previously mentioned as reasons for volunteering.

Getting a clear idea about what you want to achieve as a volunteer and what you would like to receive through having your wishes, wants and needs met through volunteering will make it easier for you to identify options and strategies to accomplish those goals.

Your two goals might be simple overall statements such as Margo's:

**Margo's Achieving goal:**
*To make a positive difference in her community.'*
**Receiving goal:**
*To meet new people and feel that she was being useful.'*

Or they might be very specific as they were for Jenny:

**Jenny's achieving goal:**
*To use her skills in teaching English as a foreign language to help newly immigrant women to integrate into the community.*
**Her receiving goal:**
*To learn about different cultures from the women who had been brought up in them.*

Occasionally, for some people, these two goals of giving and receiving might be the same as they were for Meg:

*Meg wanted to create a voluntarily managed crèche because she needed to have somewhere to place her children a few mornings each week and no such crèche existed in her locality.*

Take some time to consider what both of these goals might be for you.

The more clearly you state your goals, whether wide or specific, the easier it will be for you to identify how to achieve them and to measure progress.

# Achieving Goal

What you might like to achieve through volunteering could be anything from contributing to World Peace or playing a part in the eradication of hunger in the World; to being a more helpful neighbor or the success of your child's school fundraising project. All these and everything in between are important and valuable achievements to aim for.

Your goals for achievement might be general: being of help in your community. Or they might be very specific: establishing a playgroup; providing care for abandoned cats; helping to improve the sight of sight-impaired people in India.

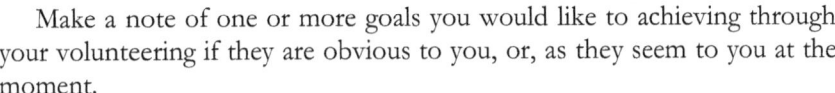

### Make a note

Make a note of one or more goals you would like to achieving through your volunteering if they are obvious to you, or, as they seem to you at the moment.

1.

2.

3.

# Receiving Goal

What you would like to receive from your volunteering might not be so easy to identify. This might be because you have given it no thought so far or you might believe that it is not appropriate to consider what could be gained or how you might benefit from your volunteering.

It is my experience that commitment to any volunteer activity is often more sustainable when there is some giving and receiving.

**Make a note**

Make a note of anything that comes to mind that you would like to receive through your volunteering.

# 4

# EXPLORING YOUR INTERESTS AND SKILLS

In order to pursue your achieving goal you will need to consider what you have to offer. For your volunteering to be most valuable, effective, rewarding and enjoyable there are a number of areas to be considered:

1.  What are your interests and passions?
2.  What are your skills and abilities?
3.  What are your experiences?
4.  What are your ways of being?

In this next part of the program we will explore each of these questions in turn.

## Your interests and passions

> Some volunteering situations might require people to muck in and get on with doing whatever needs to be done to sort a situation out. However, because volunteering is something you choose to do, you also have the right to choose something involving your interests and passions.

**What is the difference between an interest and a passion?**

It seems to me that an interest is something you occasionally engage in; sometimes think about or something that comes up in conversation now and then with other people. It is a topic you might read about occasionally in books and magazines and which you would be mildly disappointed if you missed a TV program about it.

A passion is something you engage in whenever possible, frequently think about, is the main topic of conversation with at least one other person, is a subject you avidly read about in books and magazines and you would be distressed to miss a TV program about.

**Identifying your interests and passions**

What are your current interests and passions? Are there subjects in your past that you had an interest in or a passion for? Is there something you used to enjoy doing and have not done for a while? Might you enjoy brushing up on your old skills, interests or passions to share with others?

Are there some things you would like to re-learn or wish to improve upon in order to be of help to others, such as sign language, sewing, computing, etc.? This might open up some interesting areas of volunteering for you and perhaps renew some of your old passions.

**Create a list**

Write a list of all the things that you enjoy doing or for which you have or have previously had an interest or passion.

You could start out with broad headings such as:

Music.
Art.
Crafts.
Dance.
Education.
Drama.
Food.
Animals.
Books.
Exercise.
Sport.
Children.
Outdoor activities.
The environment.
Technology.
Community.
History.
What else?

## Make your list of interests

- 
- 
- 
- 
- 
- 
- 
- 
- 
- 
- 
- 
- 
- 
- 
- 
- 
-

-

-

-

-

-

-

-

-

-

-

-

-

-

-

-

-

-

-

-

-

Select one of the items on your list. One might jump out at you. Take that one and make another list with more details of that subject.

# Q

Examples of subjects and the questions to consider:

1. If your passion is art, is it based upon practicing an art form or appreciating it? What kind of art are you interested in? If it is visual art for example, then what form does that take? Painting, sculpture, graphics, computer-generated art or another discipline? If it's painting, what kind of painting: oil, watercolor, pastel, or something else?
2. If you have an interest in wildlife, is it all wildlife or one creature in particular; birds for instance? Is your interest in caring, observing or conserving rare species of birds?
3. If your passion is for food, is it eating, preparing or growing food that interests you? Are you interested in nutrition, organic production, local production or fair trade?

(To illustrate this self-coaching process I offer some examples of lists created by people as they worked through this program.)

**Jane's list**
**Regarding her interest in drama**
Writing and adapting plays
Directing
Teaching young people theatrical skills
Producing performance

**Ellie's list**
**Regarding her interest in food**
Preparation
Nutrition
Organic production
Local production
Fair trade

Keep working with your interests list until you have found a few subjects that really engage you and you have identified the details in them that get you excited or which renew your interest or passion.

## Make your list of interests in more detail

-

-

-

-

-

-

-

-

-

-

-

-

-

-

-

-

-

-

-

-

-

-

-

-

-

-

-

-

-

-

-

-

-

-

-

-

-

-

# Q

**What would you like to do with your interest or passion for these subjects?**

➤ Inspire others to take an interest in them?
➤ Teach them?
➤ Help those who teach them?
➤ Use your interest to help those who are disadvantaged in some way?
➤ What else?

**Jane's list:**
**Drama.**
Teaching drama
Sharing this passion with other people
Getting young people interested in drama
Using drama to give youngsters self-confidence
Putting on dramatic productions
Helping those who are disadvantaged

> Note: While sharing your interest or passion with other people you may be inspired to learn more about the subject for your own enjoyment and in order to be of even greater help.

**Make a list**
Make a list of what you could do with your interests

- 

- 

- 

- 

- 

-

-

-

-

-

-

-

-

-

-

-

-

-

-

-

-

-

-

-

-

-

# Your skills and abilities

What skills do you have that could be usefully volunteered? This is a big question that may take some thought and might throw up some surprising answers when considered in depth.

> I have not come across any skill that, no matter how seemingly ordinary, insignificant or obscure cannot be of use to somebody, somewhere.

You might be certain of the skills you have that you want to offer. In which case you might wish to skip to the next step. If not, or if you would like to consider a range of options, here are a few suggestions of areas of skills to ponder:

a. Skills used in the home such as in the kitchen or garden, in home maintenance or decoration.
b. Skills with children.
c. In the natural world with animals - pets or wild - or in environmental conservation.
d. In sports.
e. In the arts: visual arts, dance or performance arts.
f. In finances: book-keeping, administrating, fundraising.
g. In literacy or languages.
h. In history or geography.
i. In recycling, restoring or repairing.
j. In IT: technical support or maintenance.
k. With vehicles: driving or maintenance.
l. In personal communication, counseling or mentoring.
m. In leading groups or managing meetings.

The options go on. These might be skills you could offer or skills you could teach.

Add to these any others that come to mind while thinking of the variety of skills you have in each of these areas. You may be very surprised to discover how many skills and abilities you have. I have had coaching clients who, although at first could only write down a few of their skills that came to mind, have eventually written pages full of them.

**Examples:**
**The Natural World** might cover such skills as:

Dog walking or training, horse riding, bee keeping or cat sitting. Surveying wildlife - birds, bees, butterflies, frogs, trees, plants etc.

**Sports skills** could include:

Competing to raise money, coaching or supporting teams - local youngsters for example, in many practical or encouraging ways. Sharing your skill and experience in your favorite sport by mentoring those who are new to it, whether that is fishing, fencing or fitness training.

**Financial skills:**

Skills in accountancy and book-keeping are often desperately needed in voluntary groups, organizations and community projects.

**Administration skills:**

Office organization and business management, secretarial - typing, filing, etc., are also essential.

**Technical skills:**

Computing, web design and management, IT setup and maintenance are skills vital to most groups and organizations.

**People skills**

Perhaps you have skills in setting up or managing teams or groups? Are you experienced in: group dynamics, team development or trust building?

Many groups flounder or fail due to lack of understanding of how groups work.

**Communication skills**

Are you an attentive and patient listener? Are you a good verbal communicator? Could you teach these skills to others or use them to get an organization's message across to the public or to funders? Could you offer listening support either in person or on one of the local or national telephone help lines?

## Make a list

Under headings of each of the above areas, and others you might think of, write a list of any skill or ability that you have in each of these areas, no matter how slight it is or how long ago it was used.

- 

- 

- 

- 

- 

- 

- 

- 

- 

- 

- 

- 

- 

- 

- 

- 

-

KAY KAY

-
-
-
-
-
-
-
-
-
-
-
-
-
-
-
-
-
-
-
-

## Valuable simple skills

You probably have skills and abilities that you don't even think about. You might be able to do some things so easily that you might not consider these to be skills at all. However, to someone who does not have these skills or abilities and who needs them, they will seem like gold dust. Even the simplest of skills can have great value for others.

You might not value your literacy skills because you probably imagine that most people can read and write? Well, actually no, many can't! You might be able to teach them.

You could read books or letters to people with failing sight or who are unable to do this for themselves for some reason - perhaps because of illness or disability. Some people need help with writing letters, filling out forms or completing applications.

If skills such as reading and writing are taken for granted and their value to others is not recognized, imagine how valuable other more unusual or complex skills and abilities might be.

Sometimes we don't always recognize as a skill something that we do every day. Or we might think that a skill we have, which we take for granted or imagine that everybody else has, is of little or no value. If you have difficulty in recognizing or valuing your own skills, ask your friends, colleagues and relatives to tell you of the skills and abilities that they recognize in you. That could help you to value yourself more and maybe help them to remember what a capable person you are.

*Clare's list*
*Simple skills in the home*
*Cleaning*
*Shopping*
*Childcare*
*Gardening*
*Growing food*
*Cooking*
*Baking*
*Preserving*
*Nutrition expertise*
*Maintenance*
*Decorating*
*Household management*

Skills in these areas are all useful to people who cannot do these things for themselves or in teaching those who want to learn them.

## Make a list

List all the simple skills you have that you might never before have considered to be of much value that could be immensely valuable to people who need them or do not have them.

- 

- 

- 

- 

- 

- 

- 

- 

- 

- 

- 

- 

- 

- 

- 

- 

-

## Two vital skills

There are two vital skills that are often overlooked or undervalued.

1. **Awareness.**

The awareness of what is happening around you and of what needs to be done to change or improve situations or to help and to support people being adversely affected by them.

2. **Willingness.**

The willingness to do something that would make improvements and to offer help and support to those who need it.

> You might consider these to be attitudes rather than skills. Whichever they are, I believe that these can be acquired, developed and perfected.

### Appreciating yourself

Through this exercise of identifying and recognizing your skills you may have come to appreciate and value yourself more highly than before. This could make a difference to your life. The self-appreciation that comes from acknowledging your skills is not vanity. Knowing and valuing yourself and your abilities will give you confidence to use them and encourage others to appreciate you.

Remember that by increasing your awareness and your appreciation of your skills along with your willingness to use them can place you in a position to make a positive difference in your world.

# 5

# YOUR EXPERIENCE AND WAYS OF BEING

Think of all the experiences you have had in your life that could equip you to be of help to others. Those of us who have had difficult or awful experiences to cope with and overcome are often the most appropriate supporters of people who are going through similar experiences.

Coping with short-term or long-term disability, physical or mental illness, getting over bereavement and other forms of loss, surviving catastrophe, recovering from any addiction or achieving weight loss can take time, strength and courage.

Other people undergoing these experiences need as much help and support as they can get. Being an example of how these can be overcome is often the most inspiring and meaningful kind of support that can be given.

To gain some idea of how your experience can be beneficial to the people going through any of these situations, just remember how much you benefitted from those who inspired and supported you through your difficulties and challenges.

If you were not fortunate to receive such support, imagine how you could have benefitted from support and guidance from people who had been through these experiences before you.

## Experiences of success

You might have experiences of being successful. Success could be in any area: creating or working in a successful business, a successful marriage or partnership, raising healthy and happy children to adulthood, developing a project, sporting or artistic achievements, gaining qualifications, raising money, resolving conflict, overcoming traumatic situations, etc.

The experiences gained in achieving and managing success can be very valuable when shared with people aspiring to similar successes.

## Jane's list of experience

*A degree in drama*
*25 years teaching drama*
*Many successful dramatic productions*
*Helping several students to make a successful acting career*
*A long and happy marriage*
*Caring for her husband with terminal cancer*
*Losing her husband*
*Dealing with widowhood*

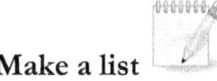

## Make a list

Write down all of the experiences that you have had in overcoming difficulties or in achieving the objectives in your life. It might be useful to also note the things that you have learned through these experiences and which could be helpful to others. As with your skills, this list can be added to at any time.

- 

- 

- 

- 

- 

-

-

-

-

-

-

-

-

-

-

-

-

-

-

-

-

-

-

-

-

-

# Ways of being

Having made lists of your interests and passions, skills and experience, it would be beneficial to consider some of your attitudes, your characteristics and the strengths in your personality, the preferences you might have for ways in which you work most effectively.

These are the two areas to bear in mind that will affect your potential volunteer activities:

  A. Your attitudes and personal characteristics.
  B. Your preferred way of working.

### A. What are your attitudes and characteristics?

Now is a good time to take a good look at some of these aspects of yourself and to identify the areas where you are strong and where you are less so.

# Q

You might usefully consider some of the following questions:

- Do you like to lead or follow the lead of others?
- Do you handle responsibility well, can do so sometimes or, do you avoid it at all costs?
- Can you deal effectively with stressful situations?
- Are you a patient person?
- Could you cope well with distressed people, children or animals?
- Are you good or not so good at taking instruction and direction?
- Are you better at communicating in conversation, on paper, in presentations or electronically?
- Would you rather not have to communicate with people at all?
- Do you like to be inside or outdoors?
- Are you a lark, at your best in the morning or are you an owl, able to function late into the night or are you somewhere in between?
- Do you prefer to work on your own, with another individual or with groups or teams?
- Would you prefer to be a small fish in a big pool, a big fish in a small pool or a big fish in a big pool?
- How easily could you serve the needs of people who may be indifferent to your efforts?
- How well might you respond to people who are very different from you or who behave in ways that you find difficult?
- Can you help people or work alongside them without moralizing, preaching or judging them?

> Our life experience, combined with our character traits, equips us to be able to deal well in some situation and not so well in others. We can't all be firefighters and we are not all undiscovered Mother Teresa's!

Remember, you are who you are and the more honest you can be about your attitudes and characteristics at this stage the easier it will be for you to find your perfect volunteer niche. And the more satisfying it will be when you do.

### Jane's list
*Prefers to lead*
*Has a lot of patience*
*Can deal with tricky situations and difficult people*
*Is compassionate and supportive*
*Can deal well with stress*
*Can work effectively anytime of the day*
*Works well with people, especially young people*

## Make a list

Write down the characteristics and attitudes you have which could help you to be most effective and valuable in your volunteering.

- 

- 

- 

- 

- 

-

-

-

-

-

-

-

-

-

-

-

-

-

-

-

-

-

-

-

-

**Above your own needs**

Volunteering usually starts with the requirement that, while volunteering, you place the needs of others above your own. This applies whether you volunteer with people, animals or plants; whether you are a leader of a voluntary activity, a project, a group or organization or you are an occasional volunteer member of one of these.

This is not about ignoring your own needs. It is about recognizing and being willing to prioritize the needs of those you are volunteering to support, above your own.

While volunteering, you may find yourself in the company of people with who you would not normally have any interaction and with whom you feel uncomfortable. You might be faced with situations that challenge your preconceptions and assumptions. In order to be supportive and of service to people, to a cause or to the aims of an organization, you may be required to set aside your own preferences, and wishes.

**Developing yourself**

Volunteering can provide you with wonderful opportunities for self-development:

a.  If you are usually a solitary person then, in the service of others, you may discover the joys of working cooperatively in groups.

b.  You might find yourself handling more responsibility than you thought you were able to manage.

c.  To be effective when working with other volunteers, you may need to develop skills in eliciting their cooperation. Because volunteers freely offer their time you may need to improve your attitudes of appreciation and encouragement.

d.  You could develop skills such as attentive listening so that you can give others what they really need rather than what you think they need or only what you believe you are capable of offering.

> By starting from a place of honest self-understanding and acknowledgment of yourself, you can be of genuine help to others, while finding pleasure and satisfaction in what you do.

Through your volunteer experience you might be able to develop your abilities, personality and characteristics or to expand your belief in what you are capable of giving and uncover an increased willingness to give it.

## Make a list

Write down the characteristics and attitudes that you have which you would like to develop or improve through your volunteering.

-

-

-

-

-

-

-

-

-

-

-

-

-

-

-

-

## B. What is your preferred way of working?

There is probably a need for volunteers in hundreds of activities in hundreds of groups and organizations in your local area alone. So making the choice in the way you are going to contribute can often be a difficult one. However, volunteer activities can usually be broadly classified in three ways of working:

3.   Thinking volunteering.
4.   Connecting volunteering.
5.   Action volunteering.

### Thinking volunteering

This type of volunteering is one in which you would primarily use your brain. Most aspects of administrating; fundraising or campaigning; communication; developing systems and strategic planning are examples of work that fits into thinking volunteering.

Issues that you can discuss in the abstract, such as working for social or environmental improvement fit into this area. If you deal easily with concepts, can see the big picture, prefer to work in the background or if you like there to be a distance between what you do and what ultimately happens as a result of your volunteering, you might choose to become a Thinking Volunteer.

### Connecting volunteering

Connecting volunteering often includes activities where you will connect and engage with people. Connecting volunteering usually provides opportunities to offer practical care, help and support to those who are in need or who are in some way disadvantaged.

Almost anything you do with others, any activity that directly benefits individuals or your immediate community could be described as connecting volunteering.

If you enjoy being around people and want to do hands on work with or for them, if you would like to be there to see the benefit of what you do and feel good about the contributions you make for the improvement of the circumstances of others, you might choose to be a Connecting Volunteer.

### Action volunteering

Action volunteering sometimes involves travelling to places where action is needed. Or it requires acting locally. (Often while thinking globally).

You might want to make a direct active contribution to your community. Whether that is your community in general or a specific community such as a faith centered community or one based upon your child's school.

You might want to be active through your sports or hobbies, within a social based fundraising group or one that makes direct social or environmental changes. There are many ways in which you might choose to be an Action Volunteer.

After considering these different ways of your preferred working you might realize that your preferences are some combination of these. This could widen or focus your volunteering options.

### Make a note

Make a note of what you have identified about yourself that indicates the type of volunteer you would prefer to be.

- 
- 
- 
- 
- 
- 
- 
- 
- 
- 
- 
- 
-

## All types

Most sensible groups and organizations will wish to attract people from all of these three categories. They realize that they need a variety of skills, interest and ways of engaging from their volunteers in order to a function effectively and efficiently.

## Recognizing yourself

After considering all of these areas of your skills, interests, experience, characteristics and your preferred way of working you might be confirming what you have always known about yourself, or you could be recognizing for the first time that:

You are unique and everything that you have to offer is valuable.

The next step is to assess the amount of time you have to offer to your volunteering.

# 6

# HOW MUCH TIME CAN YOU OFFER?

If you are out of work, between jobs or retired you have something that most voluntary organizations are desperate for and will greatly valuable – time!

If you are retired you may have the time to share a lifetime of skills, expertise and experience that could be of benefit to many local, national or international projects.

If you were a young and active person with a lot of spare time, your time and energy would be gratefully received and put to good use by many voluntary organizations.

Some people have more time than others. You may have very little time to spare. You might have a job that takes up all the working day - and then some. If this is so, you will need to think creatively about how most effectively you can volunteer the little time available to you.

You may have a young family or aged parents to care for who need a lot of attention and so you might feel you have no time to spare. However, doing something completely different for a short time each week can help you to remember that you're not just someone's child or someone's parent. You're an adult with interests that can be nourishing for you and of benefit to others.

### Stella

*Stella had three children under the age of 10 and a mother in the early stages of dementia. She spent her Sunday afternoons volunteering her otherwise unused horsewoman skills to help disabled people have the experience of riding upon and being with horses. She found this deeply rewarding. Her absence gave her husband the opportunity to be with his children and have a fun afternoon with them every week. This sometimes also included a visit to granny.*

### Be realistic
It is important to be realistic about the amount of time that you have for volunteer activities.

> A few hours a week given with ease and grace will be far more beneficial to everyone concerned than will a greater number of volunteered stress-filled hours.

Remember, it is not going to do you or anybody else any good if you commit to doing things that you really do not have time to do.

### Time management
In my experience, time management is a skill that many people have some difficulty in mastering. This can lead to a number of outcomes:
1. Some people are habitually late for almost everything.
2. Others find themselves in a dilemma when faced with difficult choices in deciding whether to spend their time doing what they would like to do or on what they need to do.
3. In trying to fit too much into the time available, some people are unable to fulfill the functions expected of them either at work or at home.
4. All this causes many to feel stressed much of the time.

These outcomes rarely leave time for engaging in any extra enjoyable or meaningful activities.

### Over-commitment
People over-commit themselves regarding time for a number of reasons: They might have difficulty in saying the 'no' word. They could have an unrealistic expectation of what they can achieve in the time available. Perhaps they need to feel needed, important or indispensable.

> Exhausting yourself in the service of others becomes unsustainable and may come to feel more like a penance than a service.

Learning how to best manage your time will be enormously beneficial to you and the others in your life.

## Making time

One of the reason's some people believe they cannot volunteer their time is the lack of it. However, I have come to recognize that where there's a will there's a way. It is possible to make time for volunteer work in the busiest of lives - if you really want to. Very few of us are as efficient with the use of our time as we would like to think we are.

Wanting to find time to volunteer might help you to become more organized, avoid procrastination, and become more efficient in your use of time in many areas of your life.

Perhaps some minutes can be shaved off a number of activities and accumulated so they can be used on something you care about.

## Flexible time

If you work flexible hours you could consider getting in to work early one day a week in order to leave early to give you a longer evening. Or, this flexibility might allow you to work through one of your lunchtimes and chop that time off the end of a working day. By combining tasks, you might save valuable time that you can use after work for volunteer activities.

## Make lunchtimes work for you

Take a packed lunch to work. In addition to saving money, bringing your own lunch frees up the time it would take you to eat in the cafeteria or make a trip to a café or a restaurant. With that extra free time, you could do some of the tasks that you usually leave for the evenings or weekends: your domestic paperwork such as paying your bills or researching better utility or insurance deals. Some weekend activities could also be taken care of such as shopping or getting your car washed.

## Volunteer near your workplace

You might choose to engage in your volunteering immediately after work, perhaps on your way home. If you feel stressed by commuting, the last thing you want to do is to add more travelling time to your day. Doing your volunteering near to where you work may actually take some commuting pressure off you. By the time you are ready to go home, traffic may have eased and your commuting time might be shortened.

## Volunteer near your home

Finding a volunteer activity near to home is another option. You may be able to give some time before you get settled in for an evening at home.

Even with the best of intentions it can sometimes be hard to drag yourself out of the house again once you have started to wind down.

If your volunteering happens later in the evening it might be wise to find something to which you can walk or cycle. Not only might this make it easier to contemplate going out again after a long day, it can provide you with the opportunity to get some exercise and fresh air. Short bursts of exercise before and after engaging in a meaningful activity might be a great way of ensuring a good nights' sleep.

**Volunteer through your workplace**

There may be potential volunteer activities through your place of work. Many businesses these days encourage their staff to volunteer some of their time to worthwhile projects. If the organization you work in does not do this, perhaps you could be the one to suggest it?

# Spending time

It seems to me that time is a very valuable commodity - often far more precious than money - and is so frequently squandered. To get an understanding of this ask somebody who has very little of it left.

Over the years, I have spent time with people at the end of their lives. Some are content with how they spent their time on earth. Others are regretful of time squandered on trivialities and wasted in meaningless pursuits.

These days there is emphasis placed upon achieving a 'work life balance'. Does this presuppose that life is one thing and work is something entirely different? How can that be so? Surely everything we do is part of our life?

**Achieving a well-balanced life**

This would seem to be a more useful statement of intention. It seems obvious to me that to achieve this balance requires the inclusion in our lives of activities that nourish our mind, our body and our spirit. Could your spirit be nourished through spending some of your time in the service of your fellow man and in some aspect of your world?

**How do you spend your spare time?**

The time left over from earning a living and commitments to home and family is usually called 'spare time'.

How do you spend yours?

Consider how much time you spend in the following activities and how that might be better used to be of real value:

## Watching television

How much time do you spend watching television? One, two, three, four hours a day? More...? Is that really the best use of your time? Even as a form of relaxation at the end of a hard working day?

When we feel unhappy, not content, unfulfilled and our own life seems uneventful, boring, monotonous, we may find ourselves wanting to view other people being portrayed as living interesting lives. We might look for excitement and drama through watching films about happy families, loving relationships, adventure, fantasy, sex or violence. We might seek to have a vicarious experience of life through the characters in television series. These characters and the story lines may be compelling enough to become a focus in our lives.

The leaders of ancient Rome kept the population content (or more easily controlled) through the strategy of 'Bread and Circuses'. Those who ruled kept themselves in power by making sure that their citizens were sufficiently fed and entertained. Has this entertainment strategy changed in the last 2000 years? Not much, except for the style of the entertainment. We no longer flock to the Colosseum for the excitement of witnessing the drama of death. Instead, we sit in front of our TVs to witness media-maintained drama and are kept entertained at the press of a button.

While we are watching we might also be consuming food and drink high in sugar, fat and salt, sometimes in large quantities. Research indicates that many of us eat more calories in snacks during these activities than we do in our regular meals. Often twice or even three times more than the estimated calorie intake recommended for our wellbeing. It is no wonder obesity is becoming one of the major problems in developed nations!

It is no longer those in official power that keep us controlled by this strategy, it is the corporations who want to sell us their products. Even when we know that TV programs are made deliberately compelling in order to make us into perfectly placed targets for advertising, we may still find ourselves hooked, eagerly awaiting the next installment, and the next...

Choosing to step out of the spell for some time each week could provide you with several hours in which to do something interesting and useful - something that allows you to participate in life in a meaningful way rather than just observing other people doing so.

## Playing the game

Do you spend much of your spare time playing video games? A lot of enjoyment and satisfaction can be gained from playing and winning games, whether that's through attempting to beat the system or in competition with others. Games can be very addictive, especially when they create some excitement in an otherwise uneventful life.

If you're spending many hours each week locked into the world of games is there some danger that you might become increasingly bored with mundane everyday activities and disconnected from real life and real people?

It might be interesting for you to consider using your game skills in ways that could be beneficial to the world around you. There may be many projects that would benefit from your quick brain, strategic planning skills, fast reflexes and powers of concentration.

### The world at your fingertips

The World Wide Web has opened up the possibilities for discovery in ways undreamed of only a few years ago. Hours can go by unnoticed as we search the web or connect with people who we would otherwise never meet.

These Internet research skills could be very beneficial if used to support those individuals and organizations without the time or means of doing this for themselves.

## The meaning of now

Instead of being controlled or limited by time, it is possible to make your time work for you! You may simply have to adjust your schedule. You might need to become a little more efficient in your use of time in some areas of your life and it could be wise to learn the meaning of now – of living in the present.

### Living in the present

How often do we find our attention leaking into the future or back into the past, which prevents us from fully living in the present?

While it is important to plan for the future and learn from the past, these are both activities, which would benefit from having some quality time devoted to them. Rather than experience them sneaking into our consciousness and getting in the way of our being fully focused upon the things we're currently doing, or, the people with whom we are doing them.

Present time **can** be usefully spent on preparing for the future, which will save time and effort when that future arrives, and on learning from the past, which could prevent unfortunate past situations from recurring. However, trying to do these while attempting to focus on the matter in hand seems to be a recipe for confusion, inefficiency, ineffectiveness and stress.

If, while we are engaged in some activity, we are also thinking up shopping lists, pondering upon what to cook for dinner or any of the many other things that will need our attention, we are not focusing on the matter in hand. Similarly, if, at that time, we are smarting at something someone has previously said to us, thinking about past pleasant or unpleasant experiences or are worrying about something we cannot immediately do anything about, we are also not focusing on the matter in hand.

> The human mind is a wondrous thing, which can be made even more remarkable through training. Everything you can do has been made possible through training your mind.

Training your mind to focus fully on what is happening in the moment is not rocket science. Becoming Mindful, simply requires determination to live every moment; an appreciation of the benefits of doing so, the application of focus and a willingness to be self-disciplined. Simple!

## Mindfulness

Mindfulness is a topic that is now receiving an increasing amount of attention all over the world. As it has its origins in Buddhist practice, it has become more frequently associated with a particular form of meditation practice, rather than the application of mindfulness in everyday life.

I know from familiarity that meditation can be a wonderful experience producing many benefits for the meditator. Even so, I believe meditation has greater value as a means to an end rather than being the end itself! It seems to me that the most benefit to be gained from meditation for individuals, for society and for the planet, is how the discipline of mindfulness, gained through regular meditation, is applied to thoughts, words and deeds in everyday life.

## The everyday use of mindfulness

Being mindful of what we're doing at all times: in our work, in our homes, with family and friends; while educating or caring; while producing, marketing or selling goods, while offering services; and, last, however no means least, while talking and listening with others, improves the quality of all these activities.

Take driving as an example of this. If the question is: What is the best way to drive a car? The most appropriate answer would be: safely! A person driving mindfully will be a safer driver than one who is not.

> Becoming skilled at focusing on whatever we are doing and letting go of intrusive thoughts, can simplify our lives, enhance our enjoyment of each activity and assist in the effective management of our precious time.

It can be hugely beneficial to do some honest calculations on how you spend your time throughout an average week. You might find the results surprising. Once done, consider how much time you could realistically spare for volunteering each month. Then decide whether you'd like to spend it all at once or in small amounts at a time.

## Make your calculations

List the activities and calculate how much of you precious time is spent, perhaps squandered, on these unnecessary, trivial or frivolous pursuits that give you only fleeting pleasure or that you engage in order to relieve the tedium of your life.

-

-

-

-

-

-

-

-

-

-

-

-

-

-

-

-

-

-

-

-

-

-

-

-

-

-

-

-

-

## Make another calculation

Calculate how much time you could free up from those things listed above to do something meaningful and make a positive contribution to the world around you.

- 

- 

- 

- 

- 

- 

- 

- 

- 

- 

- 

- 

- 

- 

- 

-

# 7

# WHAT WOULD YOU LIKE TO RECEIVE THROUGH YOUR VOLUNTEERING?

**Q**

If you were certain that many of your wishes, wants and needs could be fulfilled through your volunteering, what would you like to receive?

There is a common belief that service is its own reward. That it is better to give without any thought of receiving. I have met people whose service to their fellow man is given without any thought of getting anything back. That attitude is awe-inspiring when it's genuine. The joy that some of these people obviously feel when they observe the results of their efforts can be humbling.

And yet, it seems to me that there is nothing to feel embarrassed about in wanting to get some feelings of satisfaction from the work we do, from the efforts we make, from the time and talents that we contribute to helping others and improving situations.

In our working lives it is considered natural to want a career, a role, a job that is fulfilling and rewarding - and not just in the monetary sense. It is thought to be okay to want to receive some satisfaction from a job well done. It is normal to wish for a sense of achievement from our creativity.

So, why ought our attitude to volunteering be any different? Why would we suppose that there is something wrong in wanting to receive some sense of satisfaction from our volunteer activities?

When it comes to volunteering, I believe it is natural to want to get something out of putting in effort and contributing time, expertise and experience. That it is all right to consider 'what's in it for me?'

> Remember, it is quite reasonable to want to get some of our wishes, wants and needs met while we are meeting the needs of others through volunteering our precious time and our unique combination of interests, skills and experience.

In fact, from my observations, I have noticed that people are more willing to volunteer when they realize that volunteering is more sustainable when there is some giving and receiving.

> It seems to me that the world works best when it is in balance. In the world of volunteering, balance exists when there is a sense of giving and receiving, when win-win situations can be achieved. Receiving while giving is an ideal win-win situation.

It could be useful to review what you originally wrote as your receiving goal. If new ideas for what you might receive have occurred to you while reading the previous chapters, it would be beneficial to rewrite your receiving goal. As you go through the following chapter even more ideas might become apparent.

## Fulfilling your wishes, wants and needs through volunteering

As well as the satisfaction of a job well done and the feelings of accomplishment in knowing that you have made some positive difference, there may be other wishes, wants and needs that you have, which could be met through volunteering.

A wish that you have may be a small one - something that would enhance your life a little bit. Or it might be a big one for something that could make a significant difference to you. You may already know which of the wishes, wants and needs you have that could be easily fulfilled through volunteering. If not, you may find it useful to consider the ones explored in the next few pages.

### The wish to meet new people or form new friendships

From time to time many of us may feel the need to meet new people, to expand our current circle of friends or to create a new one. This may be brought about by some change in circumstances such as relocation, getting married or becoming divorced, having babies or seeing grown-up children leaving home. The friends we had before our circumstances changed may not be the ones we have or want afterwards.

As our circumstances alter so might our interests and the topics of our conversations. Changing our opinion or attitude towards such things as politics or religion might create a need to find people who share our new thoughts and ideas.

Volunteering can offer you opportunities to meet people who are in circumstances similar to the ones in which you now find yourself. You might discover people who share your new interests or people who are quite different from those with whom you would normally associate. Volunteering with existing groups could provide a simple way of establishing a network of new friends.

### The need for getting out and about

Sometimes we just need a reason to get out of the house. This may be as a result of living alone or perhaps when our house is packed to the rafters with family.

Being alone can become a difficult habit to break - even when we don't enjoy it. The longer we spend on our own the more difficult it can be for us to reach out to other people, to engage strangers in conversation, maybe even to pick up the phone or take that step out the front door.

Volunteering in a project that has meaning for you can give you access to people who share this interest and with whom conversation about that common interest could flow easily. What better way could there be to find compatible people than through the activities that demonstrate the values that you each hold. This seems to be a stronger basis for friendship than chance meetings in pubs or clubs.

When your life is taken up with family matters you might crave conversations with people about things other than family issues or concerns. Taking time out from your family responsibilities to pursue interests that do not include them is not selfish. A few hours a week doing something that inspires and stimulates you with people from outside your family circle can be refreshing and replenishing. You might return home feeling renewed by the confirmation that you are more than just the partner, the parent or the child of someone.

## Wanting to find new interests

With all the demands that life can make upon us it can be easy to fall into a rut of sameness. Our routine might be the same - day in day out. We might do the same things at work every day. Our regular conversations could be about the same topics. We might be lacking the spark of inspiration that spurs us to do something new.

The world is full of causes, problems and difficulties that require some attention. There are people whose interests and passions in these issues are making a big difference. With a little research into what needs to be done in your local area, for example, you might find many things that could be interesting for you to do. You might bring forth some subjects for volunteering that could ignite your interest. Finding individuals or organizations to benefit from your enthusiasm on some subject could be beneficial for all concerned.

## The wish to pursue old interests or passions

Sometimes we might need a reason to resurrect something we were passionate about or used to enjoy. The amount of time and effort this might take may not seem justifiable if it is only for our own benefit or pleasure.

Perhaps there is something you once had a passion for that you would now like to bring back into your life. Finding ways in which this renewed passion could benefit others could just be the spur you need.

This old passion might be within the arts – dance, music and other visual arts, in any of the crafts – practical or decorative, or in sports or other outdoor pursuits. Whatever it is there could be people who would benefit from your renewed passion.

## The need to fill some gap

> A change in our circumstances can create gaps in our lives that need to be filled.

The loss of full-time employment as a result of retirement or redundancy can open up a yawning gap of unused days. The loss of loved ones due to bereavement or separation can leave behind a gap needing to be filled with activity or with something meaningful.

Volunteering can be a productive and rewarding way of using your newly acquired time.

> Being of help to others could provide you with the means to find some replacement for what has been lost or for something that is no longer easily accessible.

### Sarah

*Sarah wanted the opportunity of being with little ones and young families because her own daughter and small grandchildren had moved to the other side of the world. She volunteered in a children's charity where she could offer her skills and experience with small children and be supportive to their parents.*

## The need to gain experience

You might need opportunities to gain work experience. While any kind of volunteer work can enhance your CV, gaining experience from your volunteer activities in your chosen profession or the kind of work that you will be applying for can greatly improve your chances.

Opportunities for paid work can sometimes become available through the contacts made during volunteering experiences. Working as a volunteer might bring you into contact with people who you would not normally meet in social circumstances or in your regular work environment. The people you work alongside in a common cause might recognize your abilities and characteristics and may be in a position to offer to you, or recommend that you be offered, new or improved working opportunities.

## Wanting to learn or improve skills

You might want to learn new skills or improve your current skills and abilities.

Some voluntary organizations offer skills training to their volunteers. This creates the mutual benefit of people gaining more skills and the organization having another skilled volunteer available to them.

Even if you aren't able to find an organization to offer you some training, you can still improve the skills you have through volunteering.

If people you volunteer with have more knowledge and experience about some subject than you do, being with them, observing and the copying what they do and how they do it, could help you to become more skilled. Being in proximity to people who do things well can help you to do what you do to a higher level of competency. This can include thinking laterally, recognizing how things could be done differently or putting things together in a new way. Or such unrecognized or undervalued skills as communication – listening attentively and speaking clearly.

## The need for something to be created

You might have a personal need that requires you to find others to work with to achieve some goal. This could be anything from the creation of a playgroup to the provision of hospice care, from the setup of a car-sharing scheme to the development of a youth project. You might be able to find an existing group working towards any of these or similar goals or you may feel inspired to create your own.

## Wanting to use time and skill productively

We don't all have fascinating and rewarding paid employment. In some financial climates many of us might be grateful for any job we can get. Even so, if our daily work is repetitive, boring or unfulfilling we may have the need to also engage in other activities that could be interesting and fulfilling.

Through volunteering you might be able to use your time and skills in new, interesting and useful ways.

## The wish for adventure

Many of us have a craving for adventure: to travel, to see more of the world, visit exotic places and experience different cultures.

There are volunteering opportunities all around the planet in countries where the people are struggling to overcome poverty, disease, lack of food and water, poor sanitation, limited health care and education opportunities.

Volunteering your expertise in any of these subjects for a period of time would make a huge difference to those people and give you an opportunity to experience a world quite different to the one in which you usually live.

## The need for personal development

You might be looking for ways in which to develop yourself as a person or through which you might improve your self-confidence.

Volunteering can provide many opportunities for self-expansion and development that may not be easily available in paid employment. Even thinking about volunteering might have already been supportive to your personal development. What you have discovered so far in reading and working through this book could have given you new insights into your personality traits, your attitudes and your ways of doing things. Through this you might already have gained extra awareness, shifted an attitude or learned to value yourself more highly than you did before. Following this up with some volunteer activity could lead to further self-improvement.

## Wanting to feel appreciated

> Some of us might receive very little appreciation in our day-to-day lives.

In the workplace, our endeavors may go unacknowledged and unappreciated. This may also be the case at home. In both places our efforts might go unnoticed or only noticed when they receive disapproval from others. Some of us might interpret this as more than criticism of our efforts or disapproval of our behavior. We might interpret this as disapproval of who we are as individuals, which can be deeply demoralizing and disempowering.

Self-esteem and self-confidence could be improved and enhanced by being with people, who, rather than judging or criticizing us, receive our efforts with gratitude and respect.

Even the simplest of volunteer activities are often deeply appreciated by the people who benefit from them. Win-Win!

## The need for a sense of purpose

For most of us a sense of purpose is what gets us springing out of bed in the morning.

It is what keeps us going when things get tricky. It is what helps us overcome all sorts of obstacles.

> Research indicates that having a sense of purpose is important for human beings. It has shown that a sense of purpose can keep people alive in the most appalling situations and that having no sense of purpose can be life diminishing even in the most comfortable of circumstances.

It seems that depression and physical and emotional trauma can be more quickly overcome when the people experiencing them have a sense of purpose in their lives. Even when there are no major difficulties to overcome, our lives can seem colorless, even meaningless, if we are without purpose.

> Loss of purpose sometimes comes along with other losses: loss of job, loss of relationship, loss of a loved one or a loss of faith.

Sometimes we lose our sense of purpose when we have achieved what we have set out to do. This could be anything from bringing our children safely to adulthood, reaching a position in an organization or paying off the mortgage. Or it may be a belief that life has passed us by and that we might never achieve our dreams.

Whether you are young and have not yet discovered your sense of purpose; if you have achieved one purpose and are looking for another; or you have somehow lost your sense of purpose, then you might find or regain a sense of purpose through volunteering. There are plenty of things in this world in need of purposeful attention.

### Wanting to give back

Losing a loved one to a terminal disease; a preventable accident or a destructive addiction can inspire us to be supportive in finding cures and in raising money or awareness about those issues.

Having overcome some major difficulty with the support and guidance of people who understood what we were going through can inspire us to also become one of those supportive people.

In these circumstances your desire to give back might be a strong force in your life. You may want to show your gratitude and make your contribution through volunteering to organizations that have been supportive to you or to those you care about.

> Perhaps, through being appreciative of what you have in your life, you might want to give something back into society through offering care, help and support to those less fortunate than yourself.

## Be honest about your wishes, wants and needs

Considering becoming a volunteer is a good reason to examine any wishes, wants and needs that you have that could be fulfilled through it. This is a time to be completely honest with yourself.

> If you are dishonest about your needs you might find yourself slipping into covert behavior, manipulation and deception, including self-deception, to get your needs met.

### Hidden needs

> Sometimes our needs are so well concealed, even from ourselves, that we may not be consciously aware of them.

Even if we are aware of our needs we might be unwilling to openly acknowledge them because we feel ashamed or guilty at having such needs. When these hidden needs are not met we can become unhappy or dissatisfied and either not know why or be unable to admit to the reasons.

Taking some time to honestly consider the needs you have can produce some surprising results. You may find that you have several needs. Or that you've been suppressing some need, thinking that it would be showing a weakness or that it was not okay for some reason.

You might have a combination of wishes, wants and needs:

➢ The need to make new friends might be accompanied by a wish to develop new interests.

➢ A wish to engage in activities outside of the home might be combined with a need to learn new skills in readiness for a return to work after a period of absence.

➢ A need for personal development might coincide with a need to be appreciated.

➢ The need to put something back into society may be combined with the wish to be more connected with people.

> It is worth remembering that a self-assessment of your wishes, wants and needs is a sensible thing to do from time to time. It's a good way of measuring how well you are living your life and achieving your goals.

**Make a list**

Make a list of the wishes, wants and needs you would like to be met through volunteering.

- 

- 

- 

- 

- 

- 

- 

-

-

-

-

-

-

-

-

-

-

-

-

-

-

-

-

-

-

-

-

-

-

-

-

-

-

-

-

-

-

-

-

-

-

-

-

-

-

-

# The feel good factor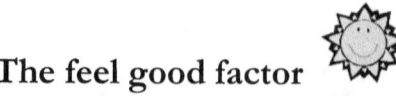

It is essential for every one of us as human beings to feel good about ourselves.

The amount of money we spend on achieving this good feeling and how much effort we put into it indicates its importance to us. It is our need for this feel good factor that is the driving force behind almost everything we do and almost everything we buy.

## This unspoken need

> The need to feel good is often an unspoken need, some desire or longing for something that we might find difficult to name or to which we are reluctant to admit.

In spite of the fundamental need for human beings to feel good about themselves, it seems to me that there are some confused ways of thinking about it. In society this often emerges as a requirement for humility, for attitudes of self-deprecation. These social expectations have made the diminishing of others or the making of self-effacing remarks acceptable.

These same social requirements might create suspicion of anyone who seems to be pleased with themselves or their achievements and happy in their own skin. This has led to many of us feeling that it's not okay for us to feel good about ourselves. How crazy is that?

Sadly, so many of us seem to have a low opinion of ourselves. Because of this, we might attempt to create this feel good factor with some form of instant gratification. This might be through alcohol, cigarettes, drugs, sex, gambling, shopping or that extra slice of chocolate cake.

It is clear from the damage to our health and wellbeing, to our relationships and to our bank accounts, that the feel good factor received from any of these, if repeated often enough, can be self-destructive.

> Sometime this desire for the feel good factor is channeled into pleasing people or seeking their approval. This can involve us in behavior and activities that are against our better nature, against our best interests or may prove detrimental to others.

We might have come to believe that anything we do for the benefit of others ought to be done through a sense of duty, through some selflessness that requires no recognition or reward. Extreme versions of this can result in martyrdom. Perhaps not physically terminal martyrdom, more the kind that creates bitterness and resentment.

## The difference that feeling good can make

> Achieving the feel good factor through volunteer activities is not only good for us it is good for those who benefit from those activities.

In my experience, people who have been helped through volunteer's actions want those volunteers to feel appreciated and valued. They want them to achieve a sense of satisfaction and to feel good about themselves as a result of their labors.

Knowing that the volunteers also get something out of their efforts can be a great relief to people who are receiving those efforts. Those people for whom asking for help is difficult might find it easier to do so when they recognize that the people who are helping them also gain something.

Volunteering ought not to be based upon having people feel beholden to us or to feel a gratitude that they could never repay. Volunteering is most effective when both those who give and those who receive feel there is something approaching an equal exchange.

> Feeling good through volunteering ought to be more than acceptable; it ought to be actively encouraged.

### John

*John was aware of his good fortune in life. He was a successful businessman who had achieved everything he set out to do and now had everything he wanted, including good health and a loving family.*

*He regularly gave handsome donations to good causes. It was his way of giving back, of sharing some of what he had with those less fortunate than himself.*

*For many years these donations gave John great satisfaction. He was happy to know that his money made a positive difference to the lives of many and felt good about himself in being able and willing to do so.*

*After a while, however, this began to have a hollow feel to it. Although his donations were deeply appreciated the praise that was piled upon him for his generosity began to mean little to him.*

*During coaching sessions around the subject of worth and values John recognized that he had two emerging needs. One was to be more engaged with people other than just his wealthy friends. The other was to be seen as a person, rather than just as a source of funding by the people who were doing the kind of work he most admired.*

*One of the charities he supported was an organization that provided support, activities and holidays for extremely underprivileged children. John decided to spend a week of his annual holiday working anonymously as a volunteer in the summer camp organized to give these children a vacation.*

*During that time John did whatever was asked of him. He worked beside dozens of other volunteers to set up the camp, drive minivans, prepare meals, and do the washing-up, clean toilets and anything else that needed to be done to provide an enjoyable and memorable holiday for these youngsters.*

*John had a wonderful time during that week. He met many remarkable people, both adults and children. Some of them gave unstintingly to make a difference to others and some showed enormous fortitude every day in coping with extreme difficulties. He deeply valued and felt honored by the friendship these people bestowed upon him.*

*He was grateful for everything that he had received during that week. The unconditional regard he received from people he respected and the love and acceptance from the children; the opportunities grow, to stretch himself physically, mentally and emotionally; the pride in himself that he felt when he succeeded in doing something he would not normally have considered doing and the humility he experienced in the face of the courage and strength of character of these youngsters.*

*He valued this experience so highly that he now volunteers in this project for a week every year. Nobody involved knows who John is. To them he is just this great guy who is willing to do whatever it takes to make the project a success.*

*When volunteers, younger than John, begin to flag, they find renewed energy through his example and his encouragement. The children who he plays games with, help to swim, to build sand castles and paint pictures have no interest in who John is, they just enjoy his company.*

*He still makes his financial donations and although there are people who praise him for that it is the mutual respect amongst the volunteers and the happiness of the children that is the real reward for John.*

# 8

# YOUR UNIQUE COMBINATION

It is now time to get to the essence of your potential volunteering by making some selections from your various lists and combine them into your Unique Combination.

By now you will have the following:

**A. Your goal for what you wish to achieve through your volunteering**
Lists of what you could offer in the categories of:

1. Your interest and passion
2. Your skills
3. Your experience
4. Your attitudes and characteristics
5. Your preferred ways of working
6. The time you have available

**B. Your receiving goal**

A list of your wishes, wants and needs that could be met through volunteering.

**Assessing your lists**

First, take some time to read through the lists of your interests, skills and experiences to get the overall picture of these lists.

It is important that you look at these lists through the eyes of assessment rather than self-judgment.

## Short lists

Perhaps your lists seem short to you. You might be tempted to judge yourself on what you see as your limitations. You may feel some disappointment or regret that you have not developed a lot of skills or had a wide variety of experiences. Be aware that there might be a temptation to judge yourself on what you have or haven't done, on what skills you do or don't have. This is not a time for that sort of self-criticism. This is the time for recognizing and appreciating your assets and your strengths.

Short lists might mean that you have concentrated on becoming very skilled in one or only a few subjects or that you have focused your attention in one or two specific areas.

On the other hand short lists may mean that life has not presented you with many opportunities or that you have been unable for some reason to take advantage of the ones that came along.

> This would be a good time to appreciate your dedication to those things that have mattered to you or to decide that future opportunities will be grabbed with both hands.

## Long lists

If your lists of interests or skills seem to be very long, you might wonder if you have learnt or experienced many things in depth? You might be tempted to think that you have flitted about from one thing to another without concentrating your efforts or taking anything seriously.

> This would be a good time to appreciate yourself for having a wide range of interests, for your willingness to try things, to have a go and to experience and learn from opportunities that life has presented to you.

As you go through your lists you might get an even better idea of who you are than you may have had before. You might realize how much you have learned and experienced in life so far.

> Remember: Along with your intellect and your emotional capabilities you are more than the sum of all of these parts that you have written down in your lists. You are unique!

## Refining your lists

Go through your list of skills, interests and experience again and this time, notice the ones that jump out at you. Highlight a few of these from each list, the ones that most strongly engage you. These may be obvious ones such as professional qualifications, years of experience of something or a longing or a passion to do something. Or they may be new ideas that excite you. Avoid judging yourself while you are doing this or wondering why you have chosen to highlight any particular item.

> Note: Keep all your original lists and notes in a safe place. You might need them in the future or wish to add to them as more ideas come to you or new interests, skills, experiences or needs emerge.

## Make a new list

Under new headings of Skills, Interests and Experience, list the few items that you highlighted in each of these topics.

## SKILLS:

- 
- 
- 
- 
- 
-

-

-

-

**INTERESTS:**

-

-

-

-

-

-

-

**EXPERIENCE:**

-

-

-

-

-

-

-

-

## Characteristics

Look at what you have written about your attitudes and characteristics. In your list of characteristics for example notice if you like to lead or follow the lead of others? Can you deal effectively with stressful situations? Do you prefer to work on your own, with another individual or with groups or teams? Etc. Highlight the ones that seem most significant.

**Make a note of these highlighted characteristics**

- 
- 
- 
- 
- 
- 
- 
- 
- 
- 
- 
- 
-

### Preferred way of working

In your preferred ways of working do you see yourself involved in thinking volunteering, connecting volunteering or action volunteering?

**Make a note of your preference**

-

-

-

-

-

-

-

-

-

-

-

-

-

-

## Time

### Make a statement about your time

Write out a clear statement of how much time you have estimated to be available for your volunteering and in what amounts you would like to spend that time, whether it is all at once during a week or a month or in several shorter periods of time.

...........................................................................

...........................................................................

......................................................

**Receiving goal.**

Read through the list of the wishes, wants and needs that you have identified that could be met through volunteering and highlight the ones that appear most significant to you.

## Make a list

List the wishes, wants and needs that you have highlighted.

- 

- 

- 

- 

- 

- 

- 

- 

- 

- 

- 

- 

- 

-

# Bringing them all together

Now is the time to bring aspects of these refined lists together for the greatest satisfaction to yourself and the benefit of others.

By now you will have short, refined lists in the categories of:
1. Your interest and passion
2. Your skills
3. Your experience
4. Your attitudes and characteristics
5. Your preferred ways of working
6. The time you have available
7. Your wishes, wants and needs that could be met through volunteering

You are now in a position to produce the interesting combinations that can be created when collecting together items from each of these lists in the following order:

1st. Take one item from the refined list of your skills.
2nd. Choose one from your interests and passions.
3rd. Take one of your experiences.
4th. Select one of your characteristics
5th. What you have realized about your preferred ways of working.
6th. Add the amount of time you have available, in which amounts you would like to spend that time and the most appropriate locations.
7th. Choose one or a combination of your identified wishes, wants and needs.

### Roger's list:

*A passion for making things work*
*Mechanical skills*
*Experience with old engines*
*A preference for being outside*
*Active volunteering*
*Time available only at the weekends, near home*
*Wishes to support the preservation of machines of historical interest*
*Needs - has recently moved to the area and wants to make new friends*

**Or, you could make a statement about them.**

### Elli's statement:

*I am a skilled home cook with experience in feeding a family on a tight budget. I want to renew my past passion for cooking that declined after my family left home. I have a lot of time on my hands now that I am retired and do not mind where I spend it. Living alone, I crave companionship, preferably with younger people.*

### Andy's statement:

*I am interested in environmental conservation and have skills and experience in many aspects of financial management, which I want use to some good effect over a couple of evenings each week - anywhere. Although I'm shy and prefer to work alone, I would like opportunities to occasionally be with people who share my interest.*

### Sal's statement:

*I have quite good listening skills that I would like to improve. The experience of my son being temporarily traumatized created in me a passion to help young people to overcome similar difficulties. I prefer to be in a support role and I have around four hours available each week that could be spent somewhere locally.*

**Write down your first unique combination**

...........................................................................................

...........................................................................................

.....................

**Consider several combinations**

Your first combination may appear to you to be the most perfect grouping of items. Great! Work with that. If not, or you wish to give yourself more options, go through the exercise several times creating other combinations.

If you are scientifically minded you will probably change only one item at a time to see how that changes the dynamics of the combination. Or you might select a whole new set of items each time. You might decide to continue to do this until the most interesting combination comes together.

### Jim
*When Jim went through this exercise he expressed surprise to discover how these randomly selected factors could combine into such powerful and appropriate combinations. He is still enjoying his volunteering with the organization he offered his skills to following this exercise. They still greatly appreciate his ongoing valuable support.*

I think there is nothing random or arbitrary about this exercise. Each item that appears on a refined list is there because it has been identified as important, meaningful or essential. If all the factors now being worked with have real value then the most obvious combinations are likely to result.

Any combination of these selected interests, skills, experiences, characteristics, preferred ways of working, time available and needs that could be met will be appropriate to work with. Some are likely to be more interesting than others and some could be easier to find a niche for than others.

---

> It is your unique combination of these factors that will make you ideally equipped for one particular volunteering niche. Your collection of these is what will position you perfectly to be the most helpful support in a particular situation. Or will make you the exact fit for a gap on a project, in a group or an organization.

---

This self-coaching program is intended to be stimulating and inspiring. It can be interesting, mutually supportive and a lot of fun for a group of friends to experience together. It often brings surprising results, and it has been known to be life-saving.

### You are not an ordinary person!
I have met people who have low expectations of themselves, who hold themselves back or who are reticent about volunteering because they consider themselves to be too ordinary.

In volunteering, as in any other aspect of life, there are no ordinary people!

Just because other people can do some things that you can do, even if they may be able to do them better, does not make you ordinary or your skills, experience or time less valuable.

It is worth remembering that I have never met anyone without some skills, abilities, passions, interests and experiences that would not be useful to others.

I have never come across anybody whose ways of being and working and whose precious time has not been of benefit to someone.

I have never seen any situation that could not somehow fulfill the need of someone who wanted to make a difference.

> Although this self-coaching process is ideal for identifying what could be achieved and received through volunteering, it would also be beneficial in exploring the most suitable career to pursue or to change to and for identifying options when returning to work after a period of absence. It could also be useful when looking for new interests and hobbies.

# 9

# FINDING YOUR PERFECT NICHE

Now that you have identified all the aspects of your Unique Combination, you can look for the people, projects, groups and organizations that would most benefit from your volunteering. You can choose to offer your unique contribution in the manner that will give you most enjoyment and satisfaction.

### *Mandy's unique combination:*
*Mandy is an experienced and passionate gardener. Her children have grown and left home and the subdivision of the marital assets after a divorce have obliged her to move to a small house with only a tiny garden. As a nurse in a busy practice, she prefers to spend her spare time quietly on her own. Her need is to be outside and work with growing things.*

### *Her volunteering choice:*
*She now enjoys managing the large garden of an elderly, infirm neighbor. They both enjoy the food and flowers that result from her gardening.*

### *Roy's unique combination:*
*Roy's combination of words showed that he had skills at, experience in and a passion for soccer; he was good with youngsters; enjoyed being outside, and has spare time at weekends. As a divorced father his need is to spend meaningful time with his two young sons.*

### His volunteering choice:

*He now coaches boys, his sons included, in a junior soccer league. He is engaged with them in soccer practice and games each weekend.*

### Greg

*Greg, a busy IT specialist, who has a son with special needs, has very little spare time and prefers to work on his own and at home.*

### His volunteering choice:

*He set up and easily manages a website for the society which supports children with his son's condition.*

### Jane

*Jane had taken early retirement as a drama teacher to care for her husband until he died of cancer. In this exercise, the list she put together were:*

*Skills – teaching drama*

*Experience – working with children and young people and living with a partner who eventually died of cancer*

*Passion – supporting the finding of a cure for cancer*

*Characteristics – initiating and leading*

*Preferred way of working – with groups and on stage*

*Time – plenty of it.*

*Achieve - supporting a cure for cancer*

*Needs - companionship and a sense of purpose*

### Her volunteering choice:

*She now spends a great deal of her time teaching, directing and supporting young people to create several theatrical performances that she produces each year to raise funds for cancer research.*

# Initiate a project

You might have identified a need, a gap that seems not to be being currently filled by a group in your community. If you enjoy starting projects and getting things off the ground you might be inspired to initiate a group or a project that could fill that gap.

It will be wise to do some research to ensure that the need actually exists or that nobody else is already doing what you intend to do. Duplication of effort and more demand upon limited resources can lead to frustration and be potentially detrimental to projects already in existence.

### Cornelia's community health project

*Cornelia initiated a neighborhood care scheme in her local community. Her intention was to prevent the everyday friendly neighborly support and care for and of people in her community from being carried on the shoulders of a few generous hearted and sometimes overloaded people. Clearly the giving and receiving of help and support can become more evenly balanced and sustainable if it is carried lightly upon the shoulders of many people.*

*The structure of the scheme was beautifully simple and revolved around a mobile phone and a Filofax. Everyone in the community knew the mobile was the number to ring for assistance from the scheme. Calls would be responded to between the hours of 8:00am and 8:00pm by a team of volunteers who each managed the phone for one day on a Rota system.*

*By coordinating calls from one central point – the Filofax - where information was kept and regularly updated, it was possible to make sure that needs were met quickly and efficiently. Having each activity and every house visit logged and the recipients confirming that assistance had been received and feedback given on the experience made it easier for volunteers to be recognized and valued for the contribution they made.*

*Anyone in the Community could ask for assistance from the scheme or volunteer their time to it. The details of the volunteered skills and offers of support were written in the Filofax. These were recorded under the appropriate headings such as child care, elder care, pet care, lifts, shopping, cooking, domestic support, gardening and so on. The people offering these would be listed under each category - some were listed in several places. People were encouraged to think creatively about what they could offer.*

*The volunteers also each had a page dedicated to them in the Filofax in alphabetical order. This page detailed their phone number/s and address, any limitations on their available time - only in school hours or not during weekends for example, and whether they had access to a vehicle. Everything they were offering was also listed on this page. The number of times their offers were taken up would be recorded on a follow-on page. This was to avoid the same willing people being called upon too often and to ensure that every volunteer had ample opportunity to be involved.*

*Although most people needed help only occasionally, there were a few, such as disabled people, the very elderly or those caring for ill family members, who required regular help. Their details were recorded in another section. Details to register there could be any special needs or conditions requiring awareness and contact details of relatives or professionals in times of emergency.*

*To overcome some people's reluctance to ask for help and to avoid any sense of helplessness, embarrassment or awkwardness in seeking support, everyone, including those who required regular assistance, were encouraged to also make offers into the system.*

*Almost everyone has something they can offer. Elderly people needing help with shopping or heavy gardening are quite capable of cat sitting or plant watering, preparing food for or visiting people who are feeling under the weather. A person who is housebound for some reason may be ideally placed to become a member of the coordinating team.*

*At the start of the project an event was held to raise awareness of the scheme and to raise funds to buy the Filofax and mobile phone and to create a fund for topping up the pay-as-you-go Sim card. This was also an opportunity for people to register their offers or needs and to volunteer for the coordinating team.*

*The telephone number of the phone was widely publicized and was prominently displayed in a number of obvious places, including the local shop and the Community newspaper.*

*The responsibility for coordinating the calls coming in was not intended to be onerous. The person responsible for the phone on the day would go about their normal daily activities while keeping the phone and the Filofax with them at all times. During the time of my involvement in the scheme there were twelve members of the coordinating team, which meant that each of us had the phone for one day in every twelve. Members of the team included several retired people, a full-time Carer, a person housebound due to physical disability, a council member and the doctor whose idea the project had been. I was the Community Listener Convener at the time and even in that busy role I found no difficulty in coordinating the calls for one day every two weeks or so.*

*The team would meet once a month to discuss any concerns or ideas; to arrange holiday cover for team members who would be away; to consider applicants or to welcome new members to the team. These meetings, which were relaxed and enjoyable events, took place in the homes of members and everyone involved would bring snacks or contributions to a potluck supper.*

*This project was not intended to replace essential medical care or to be used instead of calling for emergency assistance. The aim was to make it easy for people to offer and to benefit from a wide range of neighborly help.*

*One of the many benefits of this scheme was the opportunity it provided for so many people in the community to volunteer through it, and so increased the awareness in that community of the value and benefits of volunteering.*

*This scheme also had an influence further afield. Some of the structure of this scheme was adopted into a project that was subsequently set up in a nearby town. Similar schemes now operate in a number of places.*

You could find a great deal of useful information on forming groups and starting projects in SUCCESSFUL GROUPS & PROJECTS in the YOU MAKE THE DIFFERENCE series, which is available in paperback and e-book formats from Amazon and through our website: www.youmakethedifference.net

# Thinking outside the box

Volunteering can open doors to opportunities for engaging in interesting and creative activities that may not normally be possible in everyday life. It can offer ways of working that might not be available within a strictly arranged work environment.

Job descriptions, pay grades, limited promotion opportunities, rigid hierarchies and other restricting factors might prevent people from using their skills and experience to their advantage or for the greatest benefit to others.

## Consider these possibilities:

a. Are there things you've always wanted to do and couldn't for some reason?

b. Are there things you regret you have never had the opportunity to do?

c. Are there things that you have a secret longing to do - things you've always wanted to have a go at?

d. Are there an action, a role, an activity, which you believe you could carry out well that is usually part of a job for which in the business world you would be considered under qualified?

e. Do you have skills and experience that you could put together in a new way to be of great value to a voluntary project?

Voluntary organizations need many of the same kinds of work to be done to achieve their success, as do profit-making organizations. However, they rarely have the financial resources to hire the level of expertise that might guarantee that success.

You might find roles to fill where the people with the qualifications or experience are not available or affordable. You might discover projects, groups or organizations where people are willing to give you a go, as long as you're not putting anyone into danger or at risk.

> Thinking outside the box of limitations or the usual ways of doing things might create some interesting volunteering opportunities.

### Enid

*When she was made redundant from her office job, Enid volunteered to set up the office of a newly formed local project for the protection of cats. She loved cats yet could not have one at home because her husband was allergic to them.*

*Enid had worked in offices for 35 years and although her lack of professional qualifications and her shy disposition had held her back from promotion to office manager, she knew how an office ought to be setup and run to achieve efficiency. She had lots of experience of how offices do not work effectively; how cumbersome systems create exhaustion and frustration; how unsupportive managerial attitudes create resentment and lack of productivity among office staff.*

*Coupling these experiences with common sense, Enid put systems, methods and protocols into place that were easy for people to learn and simple to use. The necessary steps to be taken in office activities were obvious and foolproof; even the newest recruits could quickly become useful members of the office team.*

*Along with the practicalities of office workings, Enid also established a mutually supportive and respectful working environment, which enabled the volunteers to work together in harmony, encouragement and appreciation. They loved their volunteering.*

*The setting up of this took quite a lot of Enid's time at the beginning. This was fine with her because she had plenty of time on her hands and some redundancy payment to keep her financially afloat for a while. Because the systems she had created were self-managing and training was through mentoring by other volunteers there gradually became less work for Enid to do to keep the office running efficiently. This was fortunate, because after two years, one of the benefactors to the project offered Enid a job reorganizing and administrating her office.*

*To employ someone to do what Enid did for the Cat Project would have been an expensive drain on the limited financial resources of any new project. Enid's CV and experience would probably have precluded her from being selected for that paid role.*

> Enid's story is a good example of how 'out of the box' thinking can provide wider opportunities for volunteers and beneficial solutions for groups and organizations. Through this, everybody wins!

I've known of many instances where the needs of two quite different organizations have been fulfilled through an act of volunteering.

### Emily

*Emily was part of a group of young mothers who wanted to develop a playgroup in the church hall. They did not have the money to purchase the equipment they needed and neither did the church, which had fully committed its resources at the time to a church restoration project.*

*Emily had a friend, Lu, who worked for a small flower growing business. Lu had told Emily that her workload had recently increased because one of her colleagues was having an operation that would prevent her from working for most of the summer. Her employer was obliged to pay this sick colleague during the time she was away, which left few resources for employing a temporary replacement. This was going to cause problems for the little business that was already just managing to keep its head above water. However, the weeding still needed doing, as did the harvesting of the flowers throughout the season.*

*Knowing how much her church spent on flowers every month Emily approached the vicar and the owner of the flower business with the following proposal. She proposed that some of the mums developing the playgroup project could offer the flower grower a few hours each week to weed and harvest. They would be rewarded with flowers, which they would give to the church. The money that the church would save on flowers would be put aside towards the purchasing of play equipment.*

*This was all agreed to and although this did not free up huge amounts of church resources for play equipment, it was enough to encourage other fundraising efforts.*

*However, there were other spin-off benefits. Although some of the volunteer young mums had no experience of even simple gardening, most of them found the experience very enjoyable. Several of them further developed that interest within their own gardens or, if they did not have one, in the gardens of friends or relations. When the person who had been ill decided to come back to work only part time, one of the volunteer mums was offered a part-time job to work alongside her.*

*Emily had gained confidence through this process. Emboldened by her success with her idea, she approached a toy store with a request for a discount on the toys and equipment they needed for the playgroup. The store agreed to this and also donated some extra items.*

## Finding your best fit

You may have known for some time what form your volunteering would take and which group or organization to whom you wanted to offer your time. Perhaps through identifying your Unique Combination this has now become clear. Or maybe a whole new world of possibilities has been opened up to you.

Remember: seeking an opportunity for volunteering is not just looking for the most appropriate use for your Unique Combination and the best use of your time. It is about finding something that inspires you to volunteer, preferably doing something that makes your heart sing.

## Working with groups and organizations

If you prefer to work with existing groups you can research which projects, groups or organizations already offer the kind of service or support that you want to give. Which of these groups or organizations need volunteers and, which groups exist that might be in need of your Unique Combination.

Most charities and voluntary organizations have websites where you can find information on their volunteering opportunities. Lists of local groups and organizations are available from public libraries.

Many towns have a coordinating body that acts as a hub for sharing information - and sometimes resources - among community groups. In many countries Voluntary Service Organizations and similar bodies are regional or national and have a way of linking voluntary organizations and groups together. These bodies usually have newsletters, which, if they are wise, will identify the volunteer roles that need to be filled.

# Do you want to volunteer at home or away?

## At home

Do you want to be supportive in your local community?

Most local projects, community groups and support organizations usually need help in dozens of ways: start-up expertise, skills in marketing, publicity, IT skills, financial advice, group and meeting facilitation, help with graphics and other artistic or creative skills.

Of course, most need hands on help with the work and support that they offer. Many might just need irregular help with fundraising activities.

Groups and organizations in search of volunteers sometimes put advertisements in local or free newspapers. Or they may use notice boards in places like the library or in other public buildings. Shops, which exist to support charities, could be a source of information about what other types of volunteering is needed by those organizations.

You might wish to volunteer with groups and organizations that are closely linked to you in some way. These might include your church, your children's school, their sports clubs or any other forms of their recreation.

You might want to be involved in neighborhood care schemes or many of the volunteer groups who offer help and support within your community.

## Away

Do you want to be supportive to people in other parts of the world? International volunteer organizations usually also need help at a local level.

However, if you are looking for ways to volunteer internationally then you could investigate the organizations involved in voluntary work abroad.

Although many of these are looking for people with professional qualifications such as teachers, doctors, dentists, opticians, and the like, there still will be other roles that need to be filled.

There are a number of international organizations that will provide volunteering opportunities for young people wishing to do something useful with their gap year. Some time spent online can reveal any number of organizations and agencies that could offer such opportunities. Care may need to be taken to verify the authenticity of these organizations.

World Wide Volunteering offers useful information on international volunteering:www.wwv.org.uk

People with private means may be able to fund the expenses incurred in getting them to places in the world where their Unique Combination could be beneficially volunteered.

## Other ways of finding your perfect niche:

    a.   Ask family, friends or colleagues if they know of opportunities that could be of interest to you.

b.   In your conversations and emailing with people mention that you are looking for volunteer activities and ask them to spread the word.

c.   Talk to people you know who are involved in volunteer work to find out what they do and how and when they do it.

d.   If you know of people who are in receipt of volunteer care or support, ask them who offers it and how they have experienced it.

e.   Put up notices in all the places you can think of describing the skills etc that you have to offer (you may or may not want to describe them as your Unique Combination), and invite interested people to contact you, perhaps through a Post Office Box number.

**Do your homework**

While you are following up these leads find out some details of the reputation each organization has for such things as useful work, client satisfaction and the turnover of volunteers etc.

Talk to current and past volunteers, if possible. However, if you hear some less than complementary things about a group or organization from a former volunteer, remember that there are always two sides to every story.

You might discover that there are a number of possibilities available to you. You can then choose the one that is most appropriate for you, the one that is the best fit for your Unique Combination, the one that is of most interest to you, the one that you believe you will find to be the most rewarding and which will provide you with what you want to achieve.

You might of course decide that variety is the spice of life and so choose a couple of volunteering opportunities, each perhaps quite different from one another.

# Making your offer

Having identified your preferred volunteering options, you can now approach the individual, the group or the organization to which you wish to offer your services. This may be as simple as letting someone know you are available to help or putting your name down on a list at the end of a meeting or a presentation. Or it might require you to make contact with an organization in person, by telephone or through the Internet. If the role you are interested in is a significant one then you will probably be required to attend an interview.

If you are offering to be a volunteer marshal on the annual fund-raising run for your favorite charity, there may be no need to offer many details of your skills and experience. This is likely to be different if you are offering yourself as a part-time volunteer child-minder in a daycare centre or the coordinator of a big fundraising effort.

## The interview

Treat any discussion you have with the people representing a group or an organization as an interview, even if those who are 'interviewing' you don't treat it as such.

This is not only an opportunity for them to discover your suitability for working with their organization, nor is it just for you to find out if you want to work with them. This is a mutual interview. It is a two-way conversation in which to explore mutual compatibility.

It is up to you to discover more about them, what they do and how they do it and to make sure that your skills and interests fit the role. You will not want to be a square peg in a round hole.

When considering becoming part of a project or joining any group or organization it is important to fully understand their stated objectives. It is surprising how frequently the goal, the aims and objectives of groups and organizations are unclear, even to many of the people involved in them. The objectives can sometimes be a vague sort of 'understanding' among some people and even a wish, a dream or an ideal among others.

## Are your aims compatible?

You can check this out by asking those involved what the stated objectives are. Are these aims written down in a mission statement? Are there minutes of meetings that record a clear statement of intent? You might want to ask the existing members of the group what each of them believes the stated objectives are? You could also ask how the group is doing in achieving these.

If the aims have never been stated clearly or if some in the group disagree about what they are, your asking for clarity might heighten their awareness about this and encourage a process for identifying them. It might not! You may then have to decide whether this is a group to which you want to commit time and energy.

In your discussions you might discover that everybody in the organization comes from a part of society quite different from your own. This might be interesting and in fact may be one of the things that you're looking for. On the other hand, it might lead you to feel out of place.

Other important topics for this conversation would be values and ethics. In volunteering, even more than in paid employment, it is important that the values and ethics of the organization match the values of the volunteers.

Your time and your Unique Combination are precious to you. By asking questions regarding how these people could use these most effectively, you are encouraging people to value you.

Ask about the kind of care, support or activities that are offered by this group or organization: to who are these offered? How are these offered? When and where are these offered? What kind of feedback system is available to those who are on the receiving end?

Ask about the supporters of the organization: who are the funders? Have the same funders supported the organization for a long time? Or does the organization need to find new providers of funds every year or so?

Ask about the management system: who is on the board of trustees and who is the chairperson or the president? Who are the people who sit on the organizing committee and who is that chairperson? Who are the people who work in managerial positions?

Ask about the meeting structures that support the inner workings of the group: How are decisions made at the various levels of the organization - especially those that affect the volunteers? How much input do the volunteers have in these meetings and decisions?

Ask about the other volunteers: how many are there? What kind of people are they? Have many volunteers worked with the organization for a long time or do they tend to only be engaged for short periods? What sort of turnover is there in volunteers?

## Be well prepared

Your other aim in this interview/conversation will be to convey who you are and what you are bringing to this role. What you want to do and how you want to do it and the amount of time that you have available.

Having completed the Unique Combination process you will have this information at your fingertips. You will know exactly the kind of volunteer work you want to do, how and when. Put some thought into how you could best get this information across. You might find it useful to get some practice by asking a friend to 'interview' you.

## Create a CV

> In some cases applying for a volunteer post is very similar to applying for paid employment.

You may be asked to provide a CV. You may already have such a thing, in which case, you could bring this up to date or make it more relevant by adding some appropriate information from your lists of interests, skills and experiences.

On the other hand you might want to create a new form of a CV to be appropriate to the role for which you are applying. Even if you will not be required to give a written CV, having gone through the process of creating one will fix the relevant details firmly in your mind. This will make it easy for you to describe your abilities and experience during an interview.

CV's for volunteer activities can be much less formal than those for paid employment. A voluntary organization might be more interested in who you are as a person and where your passion lies rather than which university you attended. They may be keen to know how much practical experience you could bring to the role and how much time you are willing to commit rather than the date and place of your birth. In some countries applicants for paid or volunteer roles are not now required to state their age or even their gender.

### Your time

Be clear and honest about the amount of time you have available and in what amounts you wish to spend it.

Be aware that while volunteering for a cause close to your heart you might find yourself giving more time than you originally intended, especially if you have difficulty in saying no. Situations may carry you away and people can be very persuasive. This could lead to fatigue, burn out or feelings of resentment.

> Being very clear and upfront about the time that you have available prevents people from having unrealistic expectations of you and puts you in control of managing your time.

### Expressing what you wish to gain from volunteering

In some circumstances it will be important for you to be clear about what you are hoping to receive from volunteering with a project, group or organization, especially if this includes training opportunities. In other circumstances these benefits might be personal ones. You may or may not choose to mention such things as wanting to fill a gap in your life or a need to feel useful. That is up to you.

### Useful practice

If volunteering is part of your strategy for finding a job or returning to work after a period of absence, then preparing for and having conversations or interviews with volunteer groups or organizations will be useful practice for you.

However, it is important to remember that this is not all about you. The time of the people who will be interviewing you is valuable to them and their organization. Avoid wasting it. Apply only to organizations you would be interested in working with.

> If, during or after your interview/conversation you realize that this would not work for you, say so. This will allow them to concentrate on other candidates.

## Networking

The world of volunteering tends to be a network of networks. If your Unique Combination is not perfectly suited to one group it is likely that someone within that group will know of other organizations that may be more appropriate for you.

> The more clear and honest you are in your conversations/interviews the better your chances will be of finding your perfect niche

## Having a test drive

If you are not certain which volunteer opportunity is the perfect fit for you it might be wise to try out several of them. There are several advantages of this:

1. You can gain experience of these activities and the ways in which the groups and organization's work.
2. You can discover if the role is the right one for you.
3. You may find that the activities you engage in are exactly what you want to do although the other members of the group are not the people with whom you want to do it.
4. Or vice versa.

In this case it would be sensible to explain upfront that you have a number of volunteer options that you wish to try out before committing yourself. Otherwise you may come across as indecisive or unreliable. Remember the networks!

## Some factors in being accepted

Of course, no group or organization is obliged to accept the volunteer services of everybody who offers. There may be any number of reasons why some individuals might not seem a good fit to a particular group.

Whilst most people could become involved in many of the aspects of a fundraising event, in some organizations or for some roles, volunteers will be required to have specific skills and experiences and sometimes certain attitudes and characteristics.

# Background checks

There are some legal requirements when recruiting volunteers.

In many situations, such as where volunteers will be entering people's homes or where they will be dealing with children or vulnerable people, care and attention will be needed in their selection. In some cases this will require conformity with some due diligence procedure such as checking backgrounds, and references.

It is common practice in most countries now for potential volunteers to undergo some form of background check before they are able to commence their volunteering activities.

Volunteers are now usually screened for many of the same reasons that employers conduct background checks on employees. The ultimate goal is to verify identity and weed out potential problems, especially problems that could arise from an undisclosed criminal record or a history of inappropriate behavior.

## Sensible precautions

In situations where background screening is not mandatory or a strict legal requirement, many volunteer organizations may still find background screening prudent. Like businesses, voluntary organizations must respond to the needs and fears of their clients.

Parents, for example, have a legitimate right to assurance that their children will be kept safe, whether at school or weekend soccer practice. Adult children of an elderly parent will want to know their loved one is not a target for abuse.

It is important to be aware that an organization's failure to diligently protect the vulnerable and to maintain trust can be devastating for its future, leading to loss of community support, loss of funding, or even a lawsuit for negligent selection of a volunteer.

Some countries have introduced new schemes to replace and improve upon the old disclosure arrangements for people who work with vulnerable groups.

In most cases these new schemes are intended to:

- ➢ Help to ensure that those who have regular contact with children and protected adults through paid and unpaid work do not have a known history of harmful behavior.
- ➢ Be quick and easy to use.
- ➢ Reduce the need for people to complete a detailed application form every time a disclosure check is required.
- ➢ Strike a balance between proportionate protection and robust

regulation.

> Make it easier for employers and voluntary organizations to determine who needs to be checked to protect their client group.

Usually, legislation or recommendations call for some form of registration system for all those who work with children and vulnerable adults that would confirm that there is no known reason why an individual should not work with these client groups.

These requirements are intended to help local communities flourish and become stronger, safer places to live.

They have mostly been built upon what has been learned from previous disclosure and disqualification services to develop efficient systems that will strengthen protection for vulnerable groups and reduce bureaucracy.

In many cases a definite improvement is the clarity that individuals do not need to have (and pay for) a different disclosure for each voluntary/paid job they have and that there will be improved updating of information as the databases build up information.

Some volunteers are very concerned about background checks. It has been known for long-time volunteers to resign over an organization's newly instituted screening policy and some new volunteer recruits have abandoned their application rather than submit to screening.

Privacy and security of personal information are common objections that volunteers have to background screening. Volunteers may also feel screening creates an atmosphere of distrust or suspicion.

Data security is a major concern. As a volunteer you have a legitimate right to know that your personal information will be kept secure, either with online encryption systems or in locked file cabinets.

You may also have questions about the amount and kinds of information covered in the background check. Does the information to be collected relate to the job? Does the organization routinely ask its volunteers to agree to a credit check when the job does not require money handling?

Your concerns about data privacy and security can often be allayed if an organization provides a good written policy addressing privacy and data security issues.

**Your rights**

Privacy and security of your personal information are legitimate concerns.

Identity theft is a real threat. Personal information collected just to start the screening process may be all an identity thief needs. Not only that, some background screening reports might include personal details about your life that you would not normally share with others.

When being required to comply with a background security check the following are some things you can do for peace of mind:

1. Review the voluntary organization's policies on background screening and privacy. If policies are not clear, ask questions.
2. Visit the organization's web site. In addition to policies, some organizations will include information about volunteer screening.
3. If a commercial screening company is used, be sure to get the name and contact for them. You may be entitled to see any report of information they have collected.
4. Object to signing open-ended notices and consent forms.
5. Visit the organization's administrative office. Satisfy yourself that papers containing personal information are securely stored.
6. Ensure that personal information required for Internet background checks is encrypted.
7. Take any opportunity to check information on yourself such as your credit report.

Some countries allow individuals to apply for registration with government managed disclosure schemes. Some allow people to obtain copies of their own records and may require the submission of fingerprints along with the request. Procedures vary from place to place.

**The minimum privacy protection you ought to expect**

Notice and consent are the cornerstones of privacy protection. Proper notice ought to include more than some vague, all-inclusive statements about what the organization may collect. Instead, adequate notice would include a statement telling you, the volunteer:

a. The information that will be collected for the background screening.
b. How the information will be collected, e.g. through official government sources or commercial screening company.
c. The name and contact information of the commercial screener.
d. Sources consulted for the screening.
e. The period of time encompassed by the screening.
f. Whether screening will be conducted once, annually, or on a continuing basis.
g. A statement of the consequences of declining to authorize screening.
h. A notice of additional rights.

You ought also to have:
> The first opportunity to review information, especially negative data.
> The right to appeal or dispute inaccurate information.
> Assurance that personal data and information collected from the background screening will not be used for other purposes.
> Assurance that personal information will be securely stored, and access available to only to those who have a need to know.

Having said all this, in most cases, the background screening will be easy, simple and require very little scrutiny on your part. In fact, in some parts of the world you will be able to initiate your own screening process and offer the verified results for safe keeping to the organization to which you are applying.

Considering the past consequences of the absence of screening where people with predatory motives have had easy access to children and vulnerable people the need for screening becomes obvious. We all want our loved ones to be safe. With this understanding most volunteers are willing to comply with regulations that apply to everyone in their situation.

> If background screening protects the vulnerable amongst us and prevents future tragedies surely it is worth the effort and some small inconvenience.

# 10

# BEING AN EFFECTIVE VOLUNTEER

## Settling in

Once you have joined the group or organization with whom you want to volunteer, give yourself some time to settle in.

Remember that you are probably joining an already existing group and therefore you will be changing the dynamics of that group.

There are a number of things of which it could be useful to be aware:
1.  An established group of people will have found ways to get along together. (Some better than others!)
2.  Some people are naturally welcoming and others may feel shy or uncomfortable with strangers.
3.  Avoid making snap judgments of people.
4.  Take some time to understand why some system is in place before making suggestions or efforts to change it.
5.  Remember that each individual will have a different reason for being there.
6.  Treat all people in the way that you would like to be treated.

## We teach people how to treat us

> In any relationship or ongoing interaction with people we can have a big influence on how people treat us.

What we are prepared to accept, tolerate and engage with, in terms of people's communication and behavior towards us, becomes the benchmark for how people will treat us. At the beginning of a relationship, the taking on of a role or becoming part of a group, it is vital that we create the boundaries for how we want to be treated by the others involved.

A significant aspect of your life is to teach people how to treat you. This is especially important to remember when joining any group, particularly at the beginning when you want to feel included and accepted. Be clear from the start about what you do and do not consider acceptable treatment of you. Sometimes these first need to become clear in your own mind.

For example: groups where stretched resources, over-worked individuals and many people are in need of support might lead to demands upon your time or skills outside of what you had intended to offer. You may be tempted to give in to those demands in order to fit in and feel accepted by the group. By doing this you will be teaching people that you are willing to be accommodating and go the extra mile. So easily this extra mile can become the expected norm. This will be difficult to change and might even increase with time. If, after a while, you try to reduce your time commitment back to what you originally intended, that might be received with disappointment or disapproval. It is better for all concerned for you to clearly set down parameters around your time - and stick to them. You can then choose to occasionally offer more of your time in emergencies. This is then likely to be received with appreciation.

These parameters will not only be about people's expectations of you, they also include such things as your expectation of others, how you wish to be spoken to, and how you need to receive information.

Most of this can be quickly, easily and effectively achieved with a few respectful and well-chosen words addressing the concerns, such as:
- ➢ 'I prefer to be called Catherine rather than Cathy.'
- ➢ 'I would have preferred that you had told me how you felt about this rather than talking to other people about it.'
- ➢ 'I would rather we talked about this face-to-face than over the telephone.'
- ➢ 'I can only work the hours I agreed to.'
- ➢ 'I do not fully understand what you are asking me to do.'
- ➢ 'Please repeat those directions.'

> ➤ 'What I heard you say was…' (Repeating in order to make sure you heard correctly).
> ➤ 'Please send me an e-mail containing this information.'

Create your own parameters around any areas of concern and teach people how to treat you through clear communication and modeling the behavior you prefer.

Modeling the type of communication and behavior that you want from others is an effective way to influence how people treat you. Think of the ways in which you prefer to be treated or communicated with and always behave that way with others, such as:

a. Being punctual.
b. Being considerate and compassionate.
c. Respecting other people's boundaries, especially regarding time and availability.
d. Accepting that people have a right to their opinions.
e. Offering your opinions clearly and calmly.
f. Looking at people while you're talking or listening to them.
g. Speaking to everyone politely using respectful language.
h. Avoiding making unkind judgments or criticisms of people, whether or not they are present.
i. Making a deliberate show of turning your phone off before engaging in a meeting or an important conversation.
j. Avoiding answering your phone when you're in conversation with people, unless you are on duty or expecting an important call. If that's the case then say so at the beginning of the conversation.

None of these are intended to turn you into a difficult or demanding person. Far from it, these are simple ways of being and behaving, which could help everyone to get along, could avoid conflict and resentment and will be supportive of efficient and cooperative working practices. These small yet effective ways could help make a significant difference in all of your activities.

**Expenses**

Volunteers are renowned for not claiming back their travel or out of pocket expenses. You might choose to do this because you feel you can afford it or because you know that the organization you work with is financially stretched. This is very generous. However, if this extra contribution from volunteers, beyond the gift of time and skill, becomes the norm and is expected then this could cause difficulties for some people.

There may be volunteers who cannot afford to waive their expenses and yet might feel obliged to follow other people's example. Or they might become embarrassed when having to claim for theirs, so much so that perhaps it could affect their willingness to continue to volunteer.

As the anticipated financial restrictions begin to bite in the voluntary sector, it could be wise for organizations to make realistic provision for volunteer and staff expenses in the budget, and to recognize that they have a responsibility to make sure that their volunteers are not unduly out of pocket.

Some organizations are introducing simple procedures to ensure this. This might be in the form of a miles travelled section on each job sheet and would create an automatic repayment of travel expenses. If volunteers wish to re-invest this back into the organization that would be their choice and, in the UK for example, the organization could then claim Gift Aid on this.

> You could make the difference by encouraging people within your organization to adopt a realistic approach to volunteer's expenses.

## Meetings

When volunteering with teams, groups or within organizations, you are likely to be required to attend meetings from time to time.

> Having the ability to usefully participate in meetings is often an important part of being a valuable volunteer.

If you have had little experience of meetings, are new to the organization or are a shy person, you might not feel very comfortable or confident in meetings. It could be helpful for you to read our GUIDE to EFFECTIVE & ENJOYABLE MEETINGS, which is FREE to download from our website: www.youmakethedifference.net

This little book contains guidelines for effective participation and some useful information on various styles of meetings and some other things that go into making meetings effective and enjoyable.

If your volunteer role requires you to manage meetings, you can find a great deal of useful information, methods, procedures and processes in our book, ENJOYABLE AND EFFECTIVE MEETINGS. If your role requires you to facilitate meetings or events, there is a lot of useful information and insights in our book, EFFORTLESS FACILITATION. These are both part of the YOU MAKE THE DIFFERENCE SERIES available in paperback and e-book formats from Amazon and accessible through our website.

# Communication

When joining a group or organization pay attention to the ways in which the people communicate with one another. This will say a lot about the culture of that group.

**Constructive Listening**

How constructive is the listening in the group or organization?

People are listening constructively when they show that their intention is to listen and understand. There are a number of ways they can do this:

1. They stop what they are doing and give their undivided attention to the person who is speaking.
2. They allow enough time to satisfactorily complete a conversation.
3. They choose suitable settings in which they can hear clearly.
4. They encourage people to fully express themselves.
5. They listen with compassion and an open heart and mind: without interruption, judgment or criticism.
6. They avoid the temptation to give advice or fix people's difficulties before those people have had a chance to work things out for themselves.
7. They clarify anything they don't understand and check out that what they heard was what was actually said or meant.
8. They make sure that people have said everything they need to say and have felt accurately heard and fully understood.

**Constructive Speaking**

How constructively do people in the group or organization speak to one another?

This means speaking respectfully, clearly, directly, honestly, compassionately and supportively. People can do this by:

a. Speaking respectfully to all people at all times.
b. Saying what they mean and meaning what they say.
c. Clearly and respectfully stating their ideas, suggestions, opinions and conclusions.
d. Honestly and respectfully expressing how they feel about any situation.
e. Avoiding leaving things out, covering up emotions, pretending all is well or denying what it is they want or need.

f.   Giving supportive feedback about what they observe.
g.   Speaking kindly and avoiding gossip.
h.   Being compassionate by avoiding making any judgmental statements.
i.   Avoiding criticisms unless constructive and supportive.

If there is very little of this kind of Constructive Communication going on and people are abrasive, disrespectful or even rude to one another, you may feel like reconsidering being a member of that group. However, you might like to try to make the difference to that project by influencing the communication within the group culture.

**You make the difference**
Make sure that your communications with other members in the group comes from the list of Constructive Communication above. This topic will be covered in greater depth in Series Three, Constructive Communication.

It is crucial that you do not make anyone out to be wrong or bad if their ways of listening and speaking are sometimes the opposite of those listed here or if their style of communication might be described as poor or even destructive. It is important to remember that none of us know what we don't know.

Mutually respectful communication is not always a keystone in the families or the culture in which people live. Many people may not think about how they communicate. They might not associate their way of listening or speaking to people with the difficulties they experience in their relationships or their lives.

Unfortunately, Constructive Communication is rarely a priority subject in the school curriculum, nor is it an important subject in many professional training programs. It is my belief that if this were to change, half of the problems in our society could be irradiated within two generations. Until that happens, we can all do the best we can to make a positive difference to the communications we are engaged in.

---

Remember: In bringing Constructive Communication into any group culture you will need to do so with compassion and respect for those to whom this might be a challenging concept. Have compassion and respect for yourself also as you endeavor to support this shift.

---

**Self-disclosure**
Self-disclosure is when we are honest about what we think and how we

feel about what is happening to us or around us. If there is a strong culture of people being aloof with one another and keeping themselves to themselves within your new organization then the concept of self-disclosure is likely to be absent to some degree.

Trust is commonly greater in groups where people know a lot about one another, either because of their shared history or because of information learned through mutual self-disclosure.

You can make the difference in your new group through modeling self-disclosure. Gradually and carefully become increasingly self-disclosing and gently encourage it in others during informal conversations, group discussions and in meetings. This type of communication might then become a part of the group culture. This can be a powerful tool for helping a change in attitudes in your group towards the kind of honest communication that underpins trust.

Obviously, when talking about yourself, your concerns, your ideas, your thoughts and your feelings within a group, or anywhere else for that matter, it is important to use 'I statements': 'I notice... I think... I feel... I wonder... I have concerns about... I am alarmed to hear... I feel it might be better if we... I would like... I need to... etc., are suggestions of ways to start a sentence of self-disclosure.

> Even though there may be a need for self-disclosure to be introduced with compassion and sensitivity it could prove to be well worth the effort.

### Eradicating a culture of blame

In addition to self-disclosure, attention could be paid to eradicating blaming and shaming language within the group. When people develop the skill of talking about a situation without apportioning blame to others or attempting to shift the blame away from themselves, the more likelihood there will be for trust to develop. When things can be discussed openly without any attempt to shame or embarrass the people involved, the greater the likelihood will be for trust to grow.

### Clearing conversations

These conversations allow two people (usually) to talk about things that have happened between them that are getting in the way of their harmonious or cooperative relationship.

These conversations are not intended to provide the opportunity for slanging matches, for being critical, unkind, for self-justification or apportioning blame. On the contrary, they are about sharing thoughts and feelings from a personal perspective in order to help or to heal a difficult situation. It is crucial that both persons in the conversation use 'I statements' throughout.

There are a number of reasons that you might initiate a clearing conversation:
1. You want to clear any misunderstanding that you think might have occurred between you and another person.
2. You wish to clear the feelings of hurt or anger you are experiencing resulting from the behavior of another person.
3. You wish to offer another person the opportunity to clear any feelings of upset, hurt or anger that they seem to be feeling towards you.

> In a clearing conversation your intention is to have you and the other person understand what you are both thinking and feeling about the situation in which you both currently find yourselves. The language is always to be respectful and based upon attitudes of compassion for yourself and the other person.

You might wish to initiate a clearing conversation with someone using a sentence as in the following examples:
➢ 'Can we have a clearing conversation about the situation that has arisen between us?'
➢ 'It seems to me that a clearing conversation could help us to sort out this misunderstanding.'
➢ 'I would really like to sort out this situation between us so that we can work more easily together.'

Maybe a person is reticent to share with you their feelings regarding something that you have done that has upset them. You could start a conversation with something like the following examples:
➢ 'I think/know/believe or wonder if I have done something to upset you. Please will you tell me about it so that we can sort it out and repair our friendship/working relationship.'
➢ 'I get a sense that you are upset/hurt/angry with me and I'm not sure what it's about. Please will you tell me so that we can sort it out?'
➢ 'I realized that what I said upset you. Can I offer you the opportunity for a clearing conversation in which you can tell me how you feel?'

Perhaps the clearing conversation is to give you the opportunity to share your thoughts, feelings and concerns with someone about their behavior towards you, towards others or how you perceive that it may have created difficulties. You could then initiate a conversation with a sentence something like the following examples:

> 'I find it difficult to... when you...'
> 'I feel unable to... after you have...'
> 'I am concerned about...'
> 'I feel uncomfortable when you...'
> 'I am concerned that when you... I am then unable to...'

Person *A* - the person with the concern, tells person *B* about their concern regarding him or her and the affect that their behavior has upon them, and perhaps, the consequences of it. This ought to be concise and take no more than a minute or so.

Person *B* listens carefully and keeps gentle eye contact with the person *A*. He or she encourages that person by nodding their head and giving the occasional murmur of encouragement. *B* does not interrupt *A* - unless there is something that they do not understand or about which they need some clarification. In which case they might ask for something to be repeated or said in another way.

This is not an excuse for a tirade. It is an opportunity for honest, open communication conducted in a calm and respectful manner.

After *A* has finished, *B* then repeats back what they heard *A* say, beginning with 'I heard you say...' At no time during this does *B* make any judgmental or critical remarks or express their own opinion or experience of the situation.

Person *A* then corrects anything that *B* misheard or misunderstood; then *B* repeats back any corrected information. Otherwise they both agree that what was heard was what was said.

Person *B* now tells person *A* how they feel about what they have heard *A* say and offers their perspective of the situation or any explanation or apology for their behavior, whichever is appropriate. *A* repeats back what they heard *B* say.

A clearing is not necessarily about coming to an agreement. It is about helping each person to understand the others perspective.

At this stage a solution for preventing a repeat of the difficulty from occurring in the future may well have presented itself. If not, then the two people concerned discuss the options available to them. 'How would it be if...?' 'Could we...?' 'Might it work better if...?' 'I would be willing to ... if you will...' 'It would not be a problem for me to...' 'Could you...?'

Whatever option is chosen an agreement is made to keep the communication open between the two people involved in order to monitor the progress.

> I have noticed that when clearing conversations become part of a group's culture the need for these eventually diminishes as people become skilled at communicating clearly and expressing themselves in constructive ways.

## Feedback

> Information about their volunteer's experience is often vital to the improvement and sustainability of a voluntary group, project or organization.

Volunteers can offer this sort of information as direct feedback. This is when they are able to talk about the progress of their activities, of how things are working or not, and what they are thinking and how they are feeling directly to the people who need to know and who can do something about any problems.

Discussions in small-groups, teams or departments would give you opportunities to offer feedback on how things are for you in your work. In larger organizations representatives of voluntary teams could feed this information back to those at higher managerial levels.

Opportunities for direct feedback could be taken at the end of meetings and training programs and at intervals during the early stages of the implementation of new systems and procedures. Regular feedback on your feelings, thoughts and attitudes could be easily given during volunteer's support meetings.

> If the project you volunteer with does not offer their volunteers this sort of support, you could make the difference to your volunteering and to that of your colleagues by suggesting it.

Feedback is likely to be taken more seriously if it is not all negative. A catalogue of complaints and seemingly endless whingeing can turn even the most attentive ears deaf after a while. Giving positive feedback on what is working well will not only be useful to organizations it will encourage people to be more open to listening to negative feedback.

When some negative feedback is necessary it can be wise to avoid criticism that might be taken personally. It could also be a good idea to have some proposals for solving the problem already prepared. Most people are likely to respond better to such proposals if they are delivered as helpful suggestions rather than demands.

## Volunteer's rights and responsibilities

Most of the roles we choose in life bring with them some rights and some responsibilities; volunteering is no exception. If there was such a thing as a charter of the rights and responsibilities of volunteering, it might look something like this:

### The Volunteer's Charter

### The rights and responsibilities of volunteering
**Rights**
Volunteers have the right to:
- Be respected at all times.
- Work within realistic parameters.
- Be given all the information needed to carry out their roles effectively.
- Be allotted sufficient time in which to fulfill their tasks.
- Work within health, safety and security guidelines.
- Have easy ways for expressing their ideas, suggestions or concerns.
- Have those ideas, suggestions or concerns heard, respected and acted upon where appropriate.
- Find meaning and satisfaction in their work.

**Responsibilities**
Volunteers have the responsibility to:
- Fulfill their agreements.
- Be professional in their attitude and actions.
- Fully understand what is required of them.
- Complete their assigned tasks.
- Manage their time efficiently.
- Behave respectfully to all people at all times.

> ➢ Communicate ideas, suggestions or concerns clearly and honestly.
> ➢ Be mindful of the safety and security of others.
> ➢ Find their own meaning and satisfaction in their work.

## Pursuing excellence

Even though as, a volunteer, you are not being paid for the work you carry out, that does not diminish the importance of that work. It does not mean that you can turn up late to do your volunteering or be careless or slipshod when you get there.

Valuable volunteers approach their volunteering with the same commitment to excellence as they would to any highly paid job. It is this commitment that makes the difference to a voluntary task. Why would anyone choose to volunteer time and skills and then do so in a casual, careless or indifferent manner?

> Take your volunteering responsibilities seriously. People will be relying upon you to do what you are required to do when you are needed to do it.

### Volunteer does not mean amateur

Unfortunately, some professionals and paid workers in organizations and in public sector departments still look down on volunteers who they often consider to be amateur. Fortunately there are now positive signs that this view is changing.

It is worth remembering that many volunteers hold or have held positions of rank and responsibility in their professional and private lives. Some volunteers may very well be more qualified, skilled and experienced than some employed people.

However, a casual approach to their work by any volunteer could damage the reputation for professionalism that so many people have worked hard to establish in the Voluntary and Community Sector.

> You can help maintain this reputation and make the difference by helping to change any outdated attitudes regarding the amateurism of volunteers by being as professional as possible in all your volunteering activities.

# Enjoy yourself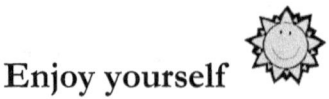

*If volunteering is not enjoyable it is probably not sustainable!*

Some volunteering is easy to enjoy, such as arranging flowers in your local church, dog walking, doing tasks you really love to do or being with groups of interesting and delightful people. Some volunteering is difficult or dangerous, such as firefighting or manning a lifeboat. Most volunteering is somewhere in between and has enjoyable and less enjoyable aspects to it.

It's a very rare activity that does not have something enjoyable to gain from it. If that isn't found in the work itself it might be found in the people you work with or in those you help. You may find enjoyment in learning new skills or in improving the ones that you already have. Great pleasure can be had from seeing the positive difference that a small action on your part can make.

Not all volunteering can have a wow factor attached to it. We can't all follow in the footsteps of Bob Geldof. Much of volunteering is everyday stuff, the kind of things that often go unnoticed, sometimes even by those who benefit from them.

Simple, easily managed activities can be as meaningful as large-scale efforts. Counting the birds in your garden for a wildlife survey can be as beneficial in its own way as attempting to prevent the killing of endangered species.

Finding some pleasure in all that we do is an important part of self-development. It helps us to live in the moment and be fully present with what's going on in our lives. Cheerfully approaching all aspects of volunteering work can lessen the stress or the burden of that work. It might inspire others to have a similar approach and it could make it easier for those in receipt of support to accept it more easily.

# 11

# WHEN VOLUNTEERING IS NOT WORKING FOR YOU

There may be occasions when volunteering does not seem to be working well for you. There could be a number of reasons for this:

1. Your heart is no longer in it.
2. You might feel out of place.
3. You could be a square peg in a round hole.
4. You may have unrealistic expectations of yourself, of others or of the role you are playing.
5. Other people may have unrealistic expectations of you.
6. The timing could be off.
7. Your skills might be being underused or undervalued.
8. Your values and those of other people or the organization might be at odds.

It could beneficial to spend some time looking at your situation through the perspective of each of these points.

Checking your current experience against what you set out to achieve would also be a useful thing to do.

# Q

A couple of questions you can ask yourself:
a.  Has something in you changed since you put together your Unique Combination?
b.  Has something in the project or the organization changed since you felt inspired to become part of it?

When things go wrong in groups or organizations it may be because some people have got their wires crossed about the objectives. Are the aims and objective that you have 'signed up to' being pursued? Or does it seem to you that the group is veering away from what you believe to be the objectives and towards something that you are not committed to?

Volunteering ought to be fulfilling. Even though the work may be tedious, tiring, challenging, occasionally uncomfortable and sometimes downright dirty, there needs to be some sense of achievement at the end of it.

If you feel unfulfilled, dissatisfied or irritated with your volunteer work then perhaps you haven't found the right fit. You might be a square peg in a round hole or expectations, yours or other peoples, may have been too high. Or it may be because you feel underused and undervalued or have come to realize that your values and those of the organization at odds with one another.

## Options:
a.  Explore your feelings of dissatisfaction to discover if taking the opportunity for overcoming them could contribute to your personal development.
b.  Avoid grumbling or complaining.
c.  Discuss your concerns directly with the people who could bring about the changes that would help you to gain more satisfaction from your work.

Volunteering is not about sacrifice or being a martyr.

There are some jobs that are uncomfortable, unpleasant or uninteresting that need to be done by somebody. That somebody doesn't always have to be you. I would have some concern about a person who consistently volunteers for unpleasant, extremely challenging or tedious work.

Difficult or tiresome jobs can be humbling and that can be useful for keeping the ego in check. When these jobs are rotated in the group or organization it can offer many people the opportunity to develop humility and perhaps compassion for those less fortunate than themselves.

# People problems

One of the challenges of working in groups is that groups tend to be full of other people!

Volunteer groups are often made up of people from very different backgrounds and who have different ways of working and approaches to life from one another. Whatever activity people engage in they bring their whole selves to it. They bring their personality, their characteristics, their patterns of behavior, the pain of their past and the hopes for their future - just as you do.

A wage packet or the prospect of promotion might compensate for difficulties with colleagues or managers that can arise in paid employment. What compensation is there within a volunteer environment for putting up with difficulties with colleagues?

Often the common ground shared by all, the concern, the cause, the reason for people to volunteer their time, is enough to hold the group together and to work out differences or difficulties. Sometimes, it is not.

If you are having relationship problems with your volunteering colleagues it could be worthwhile dealing with those problems rather than choosing to leave the group - especially if you have experienced the same sorts of difficulties with people in whichever group you have belonged.

**Options:**
a. Avoid gossiping or complaining to other people about those with whom you are having difficulty.
b. Speak to people directly about what it is that is upsetting you about their behavior.
c. Request a clearing conversation or a mediated dialogue between you.
d. Consider your own ways of being to discover if anything in your personality, characteristics or patterns of behavior might be contributing to the situation.

This last option is a useful thing to do and can be an important part of your personal development. Difficulties between people are rarely all one sided, although they may seem that way from each person's perspective! Using conflict or disharmony as an opportunity for self-exploration can be very rewarding.

> Remember, it is sometimes the people we have the most difficulty with who turn out to offer our biggest opportunity for self-awareness and self-improvement.

Choosing not to look at yourself and what part you might play in an uncomfortable relationship could be a lost opportunity to know yourself better. Believing that everybody else is at fault is likely to be an illusion. Any unresolved situation in a group you choose to leave might very well reappear in any future group you choose to join.

In my experience, dissatisfaction with the work, uncomfortable working relationships, dysfunctional systems, lack of comprehension of how volunteers need to be supported and managed and little understanding of the development of groups and their culture are the reasons why groups fail or why volunteers leave a project or stop volunteering altogether.

A greater understanding of these topics and many ways of dealing with them are covered in detail in the other books in the YOU MAKE THE DIFFERENCE Series EMPOWERING VOLUNTEER MANAGEMENT and SUCCESSFUL GROUPS & PROJECTS. These are both available in paperback and e-book format from Amazon and accessible through our website: www.youmakethedifference.net.

## Change your mind

A good first step in finding more satisfaction and gratification in your voluntary work is to change your mind. This does not mean changing your mind about volunteering in your current capacity or even about volunteering in general; it is about changing how you think.

It is working on avoiding negative thoughts and instead using positive thinking to retrain your attitudes about your activities. Changing your thoughts and attitudes to your work may not happen overnight; however, if you become alerted to the ways in which your view of your work brings you down, you can choose different thoughts to make an improvement to your job satisfaction. Some suggestions are:

    a.   Pay attention to the messages you hear from yourself and when you catch yourself thinking your voluntary job is terrible, stop that thought in its tracks.

    b.   Put things into perspective. Think of the good things about your work and remember that most of us encounter bad days in any job from time to time.

    c.   Be positive and make the best of difficult work situations. Doing so will help you to manage feelings of stress.

d.  Look for the silver lining or the gift in the situation that could help you find some good in the most difficult circumstances. This might be recognizing your need for some personal or professional development or for working closely with a Mentor or a Life Coach and having the satisfaction of knowing you are capable of change.

e.  Learn from your mistakes. Failure is one of our greatest learning tools, and yet we often let failure defeat us. Whenever you make a mistake, learn from it and try again.

f.  Be grateful. Gratitude can help you focus on what is positive about your role. You might ask yourself 'what am I grateful for at work today?' If it's only that you are working with a friendly colleague, that's okay. Finding one thing to be grateful for is a positive place to start.

# Expectation

When your volunteering has stopped working well for you it might be because you feel any one, or possibly all, of the 3-Ds:

1.  Disappointed
2.  Disillusioned
3.  Dispirited

These feelings might be about the work you are doing, they may be with the organization through which you are doing it or with your own performance and achievements. In many cases this could be as a result of unrealistic expectations.

## Expectations of the work

The work might be more difficult than you imagined or less rewarding than you had hoped.

It could be useful to think about the work you are engaged in and to consider whether it is, with the benefit of experience and hindsight, the best fit for your Unique Combination.

## Option:

You may find that there are several ways in which you could make improvements that would lead to greater satisfaction.

## Expectations of the group or organization

The 3-Ds often occur when the values of the organization and the individual are at odds with one another. Projects, groups and organizations that proclaim to be based upon strong principles and high values will attract individuals with those same principles and values. If the work and the attitudes or behavior of some people in those projects, groups or organizations do not live up to their stated principles and values then the 3-Ds are likely to set in for some of the volunteers involved.

## Options:
    a.   Some time spent in comparing your expectations of the principles and values of the project you are engaged in and the reality of them might clarify the situation for you.

    b.   You might need to re-adjust your levels of expectation.

    c.   You might choose to find another group to volunteer with.

> Be aware that if your expectations are unrealistically high you may never find an organization to meet them. Moving from group to group in search of the one that will fulfill your ideals could prove to be fruitless and deeply disillusioning.

## Expectation of yourself
You might be experiencing disappointment in yourself. Perhaps in how well you are doing with your volunteering, how much you are achieving or even if you are making any difference at all with your efforts.

## Option:
It could be beneficial to be more realistic about what you expect of yourself, and of others.

> It is my experience that when expectations are unrealistically high then at least one of the 3-Ds is inevitable.

If you realize that your self-expectations are high then this could provide you with the opportunity to develop your attitudes of self-acceptance, tolerance and compassion for yourself.

> Recognizing that we are all doing the best we can, and that if we could do better we would, could help you to find some peace of mind and a more relaxed attitude to yourself, and to others. That does not mean that you cannot look for ways in which to make improvements.

## Unfulfilled wishes, wants and needs

We have already considered many of the wishes, wants and needs that can be met through volunteering and how important it is to be honest about what those are. If you are unhappy in your volunteering it might be because your own wishes, wants or needs are not being met through these activities.

If you have not examined what you really wished to receive when deciding upon your volunteering role then you may have inadvertently chosen to do something that does not fulfilled your wishes or met your needs or even something that increases them.

## Re-evaluation

Your wishes, wants or needs may have changed since you first considered volunteering. It could be that your original ones have been so well met through your activities that they are no longer in need of being fulfilled.

## Options:

It could be useful for you to take some time to consider what are the wishes, wants or needs you now have that could be fulfilled through another type of volunteering. Revisiting the section on wishes, wants and needs could be helpful with this. If you discover that the volunteering you are currently engaged in is unlikely to meet your new wishes, wants or needs, you could then look for another activity, role or project that would.

## Time

If you find yourself complaining about how much you have to do and how little time you have to do it within your volunteering activities, then the timing is probably out of balance.

A small amount of time taken in reappraising the time factor could be time well spent. While reassessing the time factor you might come to some interesting realizations:

a. You might realize that you did not have as much time available to you as you thought you did.

b. Your circumstances might have changed and, instead of being realistic about the amount of time you now have, you may be becoming stressed through trying to do the same amount of work in less time.

c. People might be taking advantage of your good nature by asking you to do more than you had originally agreed to do.

d. In your willingness to be supportive you might feel obliged to put in more hours than you had intended.

e. You might have difficulty in saying no.

f.   A shortfall in funding or available volunteers might put extra work on to willing shoulders.

g.   Unnecessary or over-complicated procedures might be time costly.

h.   Cumbersome systems might be leading to inefficiency.

i.   Inadequate training might be resulting in time being wasted.

j.   There may be an unrealistic assessment of how long tasks take to complete.

Any of these can lead to feelings of stress.

It is worth remembering that life can be stressful enough without your volunteering activities adding to the pressures you might be experiencing.

> A reassessment of the amount of time you have available for volunteering, how you are using it, and the amount of time that tasks actually take, can be helpful to you and everybody concerned.

## Burnout

In my experience, one of the main reasons that volunteering stops working for people is because of burnout. This is particularly prevalent in the areas of volunteering that require sustained effort or continued commitment.

Any individual in any role can experience burnout. However, it seems to be most frequently experienced by people who care deeply about what they're doing, about those they are helping or the project or the organization that they are working with.

Burnout is common among people who voluntarily care for others - whether that is a gift of time to friends, neighbors or strangers, and especially when it is through a sense of duty to family. In these circumstances burnout is often accompanied by resentment.

### Attachment

*'Can we care too much?' Fiona, one of my Personal Culture clients, asked this question. In the conversation that followed she came to realize that the burnout she was feeling was not because she cared too much, although she was a very caring person, it was because she was too attached to a perfect outcome for her volunteer work.*

High standards may be admirable and certainly preferable to inefficiency and ineffectiveness; not, however, if they take a toll on health and wellbeing.

### Good enough is good enough

A group of committed volunteers is one of the most powerful forces on the face of the planet. For many of these wonderful groups, achieving the difficult seems easy, although the impossible may take just a little longer! Even so, there are times when reality must prevail.

That reality is often based upon the recognition of our efforts being good enough.

As a volunteer, it is vital to remember that we can each only make our best efforts and these efforts are good enough when:
   a.   Our goals are realistic.
   b.   We do our work to the best of our ability without exhausting ourselves.
   c.   We use our time as efficiently as possible without becoming stressed.
   d.   We are honest about what can be achieved.
   e.   We do not expect the impossible from ourselves or from other people.

> When we can acknowledge that what we do is good enough, we release ourselves, and others, from the tyranny of attachment to perfection.

There are times when good enough really means just that.

## Self-limiting beliefs

When volunteering ceases to feel satisfying it might be because there is a self-limiting belief getting in the way.

Many of us have some beliefs about ourselves that can limit our potential. That potential might be for success in business, for having healthy relationships or in our attitude towards life in general.

If our thoughts about ourselves include beliefs in our inadequacy or incompetency, these are likely to limit our ability to achieve our goals. If our self-beliefs include those of unworthiness, this might limit our ability to receive or accept love or respect from others.

When we feel unworthy of receiving some aspect of love - care, attention, nurturing, etc., there are a number of mechanisms we might adopt for coping with this. We might pretend we don't want or need it or we might appear to other people to be so capable that they hesitate to offer us any help or support.

We may be so busy giving love, care and attention to others that there is no room or time in our lives to receive any back.

We sometimes confuse being needed with being loved.

When this happens in our volunteering we are potentially setting ourselves up for burnout.

> There is a difference between finding our 'Feel Good Factor' through volunteering and using volunteering as a way of justifying our existence. That seems to be a very fine line for some people.

**Attitudes and behavior**

If you are experiencing exhaustion, resentment or burnout as a result of your volunteer activities, it could be worth your while to consider if there are some self–limiting beliefs at work.

Self-limiting beliefs often remain hidden, which makes identifying them quite difficult. However, attitudes and behavior can often be clear indicators of these beliefs. Paying close attention to your attitudes and behavior might reveal those self-limiting beliefs so that you can replace them with feelings of positive self-acceptance.

Based upon my experience and research there appear to be a number of statements that can reveal an underlying self-limiting belief. The following statements have been made by people attempting to uncover their self-limiting beliefs.

You might find it interesting and helpful to go through the following list to see if any of these statements resonate with you. If they do, you could be on your way to releasing yourself from the limitations that these beliefs create.

**Example statements of attitudes and behavior indicating some self-limiting belief:**
**Attitudes and behavior:**
I judge everything that I do, say or think with harshness. I am never approving of or satisfied with myself.
> **Self-limiting belief:**
> I need to be perfect all the time to be okay.
> **Releasing affirmation:**
> I appreciate and approve of myself at all times.

**Attitudes and behavior:**
I feel good about myself only when everybody else is doing okay. I feel guilty if others are having a hard time and I am not helping.
> **Self-limiting belief:**
> I am responsible for other people's feelings and behavior.
> **Releasing affirmation:**
> I am only responsible for my own feelings and behavior.

**Attitudes and behavior:**
I choose opportunities and relationships where I nurture others, although I rarely receive nurturing myself. I put other people's needs and desires first. I feel guilty if I take time just for me. I can be there for everybody except for myself.
> **Self-limiting belief:**
> I have to be needed by others in order to be loved and feel worthwhile.
> **Releasing affirmation:**
> I am worthy of love without having to earn it.

**Attitudes and behavior:**
I am fearful of other people's responses to my feelings. I worry about what people think of me. I ignore my values and feelings in order to feel accepted by others'. I feel small and powerless, and often feel resentful.
> **Self-limiting belief:**
> I don't have the right to my feelings.
> **Releasing affirmation:**
> I have the right to experience my feelings.

**Attitudes and behavior:**
I try to please others in order to be accepted. I can't let others really know me because they wouldn't like me if they did. I have difficulty acknowledging good qualities in myself.
> **Self-limiting belief:**
> I am worthless.

**Releasing affirmation:**
I am a loveable person and accept myself just as I am.

**Attitudes and behavior:**
My peace of mind is determined by how others are behaving. I am always the peacekeeper, smoothing over any conflict.
   **Self-limiting belief:**
   To be happy I need to dictate other people's behavior.
   **Releasing affirmation:**
   I accept people just as they are.

**Attitudes and behavior:**
I think that I always must justify myself. No matter what I do, I don't feel good enough. I'm always taking on tasks and projects in order to feel some sense of self-esteem. I am prone to work too hard. I'm afraid that if I let my guard down, someone will find out how incompetent I am; that I am a fraud.
   **Self-limiting belief:**
   I am inadequate.
   **Releasing affirmation:**
   I am good enough and worthy of respect just the way I am.

Most of us experience some of these attitudes and behavior occasionally. We might sometimes doubt our abilities or feel we could do better. However, being consistently self-deprecating or berating ourselves for not being good enough or worthy of respect is engaging in a form of self-harm.

> Note: This process of transforming negative self-messages into positive ones can be beneficial in any circumstances, not only in volunteering.

The Guide to LISTENING TO OURSELVES, which is FREE to download from our website: www.youmakethedifference.net/free-guides.html is intended to help to transform any negative self-messages into positive, supportive and affirming ones.

# Replenishing yourself

As a volunteer, it is your responsibility to take care of yourself and to find the ways in which to replenish yourself from time to time.

> It is important to remember that nothing can be poured out of an empty bottle!

## Characteristics of the self-replenishing volunteer
a. I keep in mind that becoming depleted is wasteful.
b. I can receive as well as give.
c. I accept support.
d. I believe that I matter and can make a difference without being indispensable.
e. I know and own both my influence and my limitations.
f. I trust that others can survive without me.
g. I invest in healthy personal relationships.
h. I can say 'no' or 'not now.'
i. I make my own life meaningful to me.
j. I take responsibility for my own needs.
k. I take care of my health and wellbeing.
l. I allow myself to grieve my own losses.
m. I take responsibility for my thoughts, words and actions.
n. I take responsibility for my behavior and for being assertive rather than passive or aggressive.
o. I follow my interests, passions and joy.

The following statement (source unknown) nicely sums up a healthy attitude to volunteering.

*'I can be most present and helpful by being close enough to the fire to feel the heat and yet separate or distant enough to not be scorched or need to flee.'*

## Sustaining yourself as an effective volunteer

This is your responsibility. It is up to you to handle your time well and take care of your health, your wellbeing and your energy levels. This may not always be your priority when you are working on a project about which you care deeply.

However, there will be plenty of signs warning you of any impending exhaustion, to which you can learn to pay attention. Everyone is an individual and your signs may be different to those of other people.

The beauty of living in the 'now' is that it requires us to be self-aware. The benefit of being consciously aware of the state of our bodies, minds and emotions is that it brings us present to each moment.

> The advantage of working closely with others in groups is that we can look out for one another.

**Awareness**

You can learn to notice signs of tiredness and depletion in your friends and colleagues and support them to take care of themselves. You can tell the people with whom you volunteer what signs of burnout to look out for in you and take notice of them when they suggest that you take care of yourself and when they are attempting to be supportive of your wellbeing.

Also, a little time spent on raising your awareness of things that might exhaust you, deplete your energy or lead to burnout could be time well spent.

It is important to have strategies for replenishing yourself from time to time, especially when dealing with tricky situations or with people in distressing circumstances. These might be simple things:

a.  A period of relaxation.

b.  Getting some fresh air.

c.  Closing your eyes for a couple of minutes.

d.  15 to 20 minutes meditation.

e.  It may require you to alter your schedule, the times or the order in which you do things.

f.  You may need to take a longer break from what you're doing to recharge your batteries.

g.  Engaging in leisure activities that offer a change of pace, take your mind off your volunteer work for a while or help you to relax might be all you need to feel replenished and renewed.

h.  So might be doing something nice for yourself.

You are the person responsible for making any positive difference to your volunteering. Just as you are the person to make the most positive difference to the other areas of your life!

The following exercise could make the difference to your remaining volunteering with a group or an organization, or not doing so; or in continuing to volunteer at all!:

### Make a note

Write down six things that you are inclined to do that lead to tiredness, depletion or burnout.

**1.**

**2.**

**3.**

**4.**

**5.**

**6.**

### Make a note

Write down six things that you will do to replenish yourself.

1.

2.

3.

4.

5.

6.

# 12

# HAPPY ENDINGS

If you have found the perfect niche for your unique combination, you might be pleased to volunteer with that project or organization for many happy years. Especially where the culture in your group is one of mutual support, constructive communication and dealing directly and immediately with anything that threatens to upset group cohesion.

Even so, there may come a time when you will feel it necessary to cease your volunteering with a project or a group. This may be due to a change in your personal circumstances or you might feel that you have achieved what you set out to do in the project and it is now time to move on.

Your decision to leave might be as a result of realizing that you have not found your perfect niche. Not everyone fits well into a particular group and with your current group it might have taken a while for that to become apparent to you.

Perhaps your enthusiasm for the project has diminished for some reason.

Maybe the emphasis of the work has changed, the people you enjoyed working with have left or you are no longer getting sufficient feelings of satisfaction or fulfillment from your engagement with the organization.

It might be because of some difficulties within the project or group that have not been sorted out in the way you would have liked.

Perhaps the behavior of some people in the organization or their attitude towards you is what makes it feel inappropriate to you to remain involved.

> If some unresolved difficulty is the reason for your leaving it ought not to come as a complete surprise to the others in the group.

As discussed in the previous pages there will have been ample opportunities to bring whatever difficulty you have been experiencing out into the open for discussion within the group or with those with whom you have had difficulties. Even so, with the best will in the world it is not always possible to sort things out satisfactorily and you may decide that you can no longer remain an active member of that group.

## Leaving responsibly

Be honest about your reasons for leaving.

If you choose to withdraw your volunteering, to leave any group or project where you are unhappy, whether or not you have attempted to resolve the situation, be honest with others involved about your reasons for leaving. When doing so avoid accusing, blaming or shaming any people with whom you have had difficulties.

Use 'I' statements to get across your reasons for leaving. When done with integrity and compassion for all concerned this may lead to greater awareness within the group and might leave the door open for your return sometime in the future.

### Giving notice
Unless your volunteering is obviously on a casual basis, it is up to you to give reasonable notice of your intention to cease volunteering with your current group, project or organization. This notice needs to give ample time for you to be replaced without causing a hitch with the work.

One of the things that give volunteering a reputation for amateurism is a tendency for casualness among some volunteers regarding their decisions to leave roles, projects or groups.

Whatever your reason for leaving, it is your responsibility to make sure that you do not let people down. It is your responsibility to ensure that the project that you had enough enthusiasm to support in the beginning now does not suffer in any way because that support is at an end.

Remember: Even if you feel hurt or angry as a result of the way some colleagues have behaved towards you, that is no reason for the project itself to be damaged or for those who it is intended to help to be disadvantaged.

> You can make the difference to your group or project by being willing to stay long enough to train your replacement or, at the very least, to bring him or her up to speed.

**Leaving with a bang or a whimper**
When leaving a group because of some difficult situation within it, there might be a temptation to do one of several things:

1. Leave angrily, slamming the door (real or metaphorical) behind you.
2. Pretend that there is nothing wrong and you are leaving for purely personal reasons.
3. Send a letter of resignation, which details in acerbic (bitter or critical) language the reasons for your leaving.
4. Send a letter of resignation, which is vague and ambiguous giving no specific details of your reasons for leaving.
5. Leave quietly and hope that nobody notices, until it's too late.
6. Just not turn up to volunteer one day, never go back and offer no explanation.
7. Grumble and gossip about the shortcomings of the group with others after you have left.

Any of these can create hurt or confusion, bewilderment or misunderstanding. All of them will lead to a sense of incompletion for you and the other members of the group. None of them are necessary.

# Clearing conversations

Even at the last-minute, it could be beneficial for you to have a clearing conversation with the person or people with whom you are upset, with the person who manages the project or with the whole group. This may help you to change your mind and stay involved.

In extreme circumstances a person not directly involved in the situation could mediate the conversation.

If it feels too late for this then request a completion clearing with the project or group leader or with some or all of the group.

## Completion clearings

These are clearing conversations that allow people to end their involvement in a situation with some grace and leave with a sense of completion for themselves and the others involved.

This is not intended to be a last opportunity for a slanging match or for throwing around accusations and unkind criticism.

> All clearing conversations, including completion clearings are conducted in 'I statements'.

## Step 1.

As the person who has initiated the conversation, you begin by offering some appreciation for some things that you have enjoyed during your time with the project. There are bound to be some things and it would be helpful for you to leave remembering what they are. 'I really appreciate the…' 'I have enjoyed…'

You could start the dialogue by appreciating the group or individuals for the work that they do and for the difference that the project makes to people.

Make this appreciation specific and detailed. Not only will this let people know exactly what you value, it could encourage them to be equally specific and detailed when giving you their feedback on their experience of working with you.

## Step 2.

Then you continue by giving your reasons for leaving. 'I feel unable to…' 'I no longer wish to…' 'I am unhappy with the situation regarding…'

If people know that you are leaving because you are unhappy with something or someone within the project then this type of clearing conversation could provide an opportunity for all those involved to talk about it.

If self-disclosure or opportunities for regular feedback are not strong elements within the culture of the group, people may not know why you are leaving. If this were the case then a completion clearing would give them the opportunity to find out.

> This completion clearing conversation may be your last opportunity to communicate clearly and honestly the reason for this step being necessary for you.

It can also be very useful for the ongoing development of a project or a group for you to give direct and open feedback of your experiences of it. This might be your last opportunity to offer the beneficial service of candid feedback to those involved. This can be done with kindness and with the intention to heal rather than hurt.

## Having courage

It can take courage to be honest at this stage about something that has been upsetting for you, especially when you have not previously disclosed it and particularly if you have denied there has been anything you have been unhappy about. You will have a need for compassion for those involved, and for yourself.

## Step 3.

End your part of the completion clearing conversation by saying one more thing that is positive that you appreciate or value about the project, the people within it and/or your time spent with them.

(These three steps are based upon a form of feedback that is sometimes referred to as a Feedback Sandwich.)

## Step 4.

Having shared your thoughts and feelings you could let the person or the group know that you are now open to their feedback on what you have told them.

Hopefully, your modeling of a respectful and compassionate completion clearing conversation will have taught them how to give you respectful and compassionate feedback on what you have said to them, using their own 'I' statements.

If they are unable to offer their feedback respectfully, this will either be because they don't know how to do so or because what you have said to them has taken them by surprise.

Even when the feedback to you is done respectfully, it may take strength of character to listen to what people say in these circumstances. And yet, this may well be worth it as there could be some beneficial learning in it for you.

## Completing the completion

If you feel unable to take that last step, the healing opportunities of this clearing process are likely to be limited. The others involved may feel incomplete with you because they have had no chance to express themselves and share their perspective with you.

You may feel incomplete because you do not fully know how they have perceived you or how your communication has been received. In this case your leaving may still be a source of hurt for you and for some of those involved.

Going through a completion conversation can help you to move on and help the people in your group to release you with some dignity and mutual appreciation.

# Completion and release

When leaving for other reasons, ensure, whenever possible, that you end your involvement with any project or group feeling that it has been time well spent. That you have made some difference, you have gained something from the experience and feel appreciation for the people you have worked with.

Your colleagues are likely to want to ensure that you feel appreciated for your efforts and that you have made a positive difference to the project and to the group.

> Engaging in a process of completion will allow you and all of those involved an opportunity for mutual appreciation and the offering of good wishes.

## Process of completion

This might take place on the day of your leaving or very close to it. An open invitation could be made to include anyone who would care to attend.

These affairs are sometimes managed by a facilitator or some kind of master of ceremonies and could be expected to take around an hour, perhaps a little longer if the group is large or you have been involved for a long time.

## Stage A.

Everyone is seated in a circle so that they can see everyone else. The facilitator asks you to start the process by speaking about your time with the group. This can include anything that you would like to say: such as the highs and lows, some short anecdotes – touching or humorous, and an appreciation of the value of the project and of the people involved.

**Stage B.**

It is now the turn of the other people to speak appreciatively about you and about your time with them. Not everyone will need or perhaps want to say something. However, enough time ought to be allowed for most of the people present to speak for a minute or two.

**Stage C.**

When the facilitator has ascertained that no one else wishes to speak he or she could round up the proceedings by also saying something about you.

You might like to then be given the opportunity for a brief response to what you've heard.

---

Remember: If the completion process is not something that is part of the culture of your group you can make the difference to the way people leave it by introducing this process.

---

## Celebrate!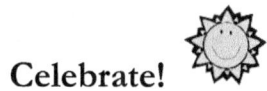

Mark your leaving with a celebration.

In most organizations the team that someone has been working with will organize a goodbye party for them or perhaps encourage everyone in the group to go out for lunch together. At the very least, they will arrange for a special cake or some such treat to arrive during your last tea break.

If this is not your group's usual practice you could make the difference to the culture by organizing these types of occasions when others leave.

If that has not been possible for some reason then you could at least arrange to mark your own leaving with some form of celebration of the time you have spent with the project or group.

# In conclusion

In the world of volunteering, you make the difference, just by turning up!

By turning up, having read this book, you now have the capacity to become an extremely valuable volunteer.

You will be aware of all the things that you can offer, how best you can offer them and when and where.

You will be conscious of what goes into being an effective and valuable volunteer and how to work cooperatively and supportively with other people.

The skills, information and insights that you would now bring to any project will be very valuable and could significantly increase its chances of success.

You will inevitably be making the difference by playing your part whether you occasionally help with some project or you contribute hours of dedicated service each week to a group or an organization.

And, most importantly, in whichever way you now choose to volunteer, you will be able to do so enjoyably.

Without your unique piece, the jigsaw puzzle of volunteering will be incomplete.

# POSTSCRIPT

## Why the need for more volunteers?

Following the publication of the first edition of this book I received feedback from some people who felt that I had not stated clearly enough the grave situation that many people in both developed and newly emerging countries and economies are facing. That I had not emphasized sufficiently how essential volunteering has become to many aspects of most societies and how the urgent need for more volunteers is inevitably going to increase.

In response to this I offer my following views on the reasons for this increased need for volunteers that is based upon my experience, research and observation.

Despite the legions of people already committing their time, talents and experience to voluntary activities, there is a need for many more. This need can only increase as most nations experience years of social change and economic uncertainty. For societies to continue to function moderately well and with some positivity under these circumstances there will be a growing need for many more of us to take some measure of personal responsibility for what happens around us in our communities and in the wider world.

> Now is the time for recognizing that we are each a part of society rather than an observer of it and that this is the time to participate in creating the solutions rather than accepting society's problems or making more of them.

A great many services and activities that help to improve the circumstances of those who are vulnerable, underprivileged or facing difficulties are overloaded and are under threat. It seems to me that the main three reasons for this overload are: science, expectation and economics. These three factors combine to make increased volunteering not just desirable, they make it essential.

### Science

Due to medical advancement, people in the better-resourced countries are living longer. Babies born with previously life-threatening conditions are now surviving; most childhood illnesses are no longer fatal; many diseases that might have been terminal are now treatable, and because of healthier lifestyles, elderly people are living to a much greater age. All of these put increasing pressure on society, especially the health and social services.

Through global communications and information technology we

become immediately aware of calamities, natural or man-made, as they occur anywhere on the planet. This leads to demand for remedial or supportive action from governments and aid agencies.

## Expectation

Socially responsible nations now commit to a level of care in their societies that leads citizens to expect to be looked after from cradle to grave. A growing number of people are requiring and expecting ever greater support and intervention in their lives to deal with issues arising from factors such as the widening gap between rich and poor, rampant consumerism, decreasing levels of self-esteem, lack of self-discipline, increasing addiction, violence and family breakdown.

Many physical, mental or emotional conditions that in the past would have required the sufferer to be hospitalized, institutionalized or incarcerated are now being handled at home or in situations that come under the heading of 'care in the community'.

People in nations that focus more on personal gain than on social equality and environmental responsibility experience the inevitable social and environmental consequences of that focus. This focus occurs both in some highly developed and in many underdeveloped countries.

Whether it's caring for the health and wellbeing of people and animals, the sustainability of the natural environment or the solving of local, national or international problems, there is an increasing expectation that somebody somewhere will do something about it. And indeed they often do! Over the past half-century thousands of government departments and independent organizations have been created or dedicated to making a positive difference to those areas.

## Economics

To continue to meet their commitments and to fulfill expectations, these departments and organizations are likely to require ever-greater amounts of money. Unfortunately, in many cases, the amount of public and private funds available to support them has been reduced in the global economic chaos resulting from the banking crisis in 2008. This situation is likely to continue for the foreseeable future and might worsen as governments and financial institutions rethink how and to whom money is to be distributed.

Perhaps all this was inevitable. I have long wondered how the exponential growth in areas of medical and social care and international intervention were to be sustained, especially in those economies potentially lacking in sustainable economic growth.

To provide for the level of social care that is desired or expected by their citizens, nations would be wise to develop attitudes towards taxation and social responsibility that exists in most Scandinavian countries. How likely is this to happen in some societies in the near future?

## Rethinking

With some rethinking, streamlining and the implementation of more efficient working practices, some care service agencies might be able to meet enough of their targets to avert disaster. Even so, it seems likely that an increasing amount of this work might need to be provided by more groups and organizations in the Voluntary and Community Sector.

It is in these areas, that some people describe as non-essential, where the most need for voluntary activity is likely to be:

> Those everyday caring actions that were traditionally carried out by family, friends and neighbors to make the difference between a person living and just existing.
> Those small things that support and encourage people living in difficult circumstances.
> Those activities that could prevent people from feeling alone, isolated or despairing.
> The support of those who provide care for relatives.
> The maintenance of health and wellbeing.
> The development of talent and creativity.
> Initiatives beneficial to the development of youngsters.

More volunteer help will be needed to offer support to vulnerable people: children at risk, the elderly, misguided or abandoned young people and people who find themselves homeless. Also, greater involvement will be required in other areas such as the environment, local economics, historic conservation and animal protection, to name only a few.

# Why now?

Even when we know that something needs to be done, many of us might delay doing anything about it, sometimes until it's too late. Putting off making changes or taking action is understandable, especially if these are likely to be difficult or uncomfortable. And yet, how does this help? Delaying is likely to make most situations worse.

Ignoring problems with health, with financial situations, with work or difficulties within the community will not solve them. Situations within society, as with relationships between people, small misunderstandings can lead to great rifts if not sorted out as soon as possible. Resentment festers, anger expands and disappointment deepens when left unattended.

How does ignoring these things help? Pretending that problems don't exist is not going to make them go away. Whilst it is beneficial to have a positive attitude, hoping for some intervention by somebody else or some miracle to make everything better is not being very realistic. It might also be relinquishing responsibility in the hope that things will get better.

> In my experience, hope, without action, usually remains just that – hope!

Procrastination is never part of the solution; it is usually part of the problem. Looking back over recent history it is easy to see examples of this.

a. If Sir Bob had not created or had delayed his Live Aid Concerts and projects then clearly many more thousands of people would have died.

b. If the recommendations for slowing down the production of greenhouse gases had been taken when they were first made in the late 1980s and early 1990s, the world might not now be experiencing the devastating results of Global Warming. While it is still a matter of speculation among some people, it is becoming apparent to the majority of aware people that the expression Climate Change is something of a cop-out in that it indicates a cycle of natural events over which we have no control. Global Warming is really what is taking place and human actions are contributing to it. Human ingenuity can do something about slowing down the process – if we get on with it! With enough time, we may even find ways of reversing the process. We all need to engage in the methods that have been identified which might give us that time.

c. If some action needs to be taken, if some change will be beneficial, then the sooner these happen, the better.

It is worth remembering that when something really needs to be done the wisest choice is to do it now!

**Financial fallout**

There are many areas in society that are reeling from the aftermath of the global financial crises that occurred in 2008.

It is clear that many people have been, or are going to be, detrimentally affected by this situation through no fault of their own. Families struggling on low incomes, those attempting to get or pay their mortgages, people requiring loans to start or improve their businesses, projects needing financial support, are likely to feel the financial rug being pulled from underneath them. Many people, around the age of retirement, have seen their financial situation badly affected by these circumstances. A lifetime of saving and the careful planning of pensions have been undermined by these events.

In situations like these, there is often a great temptation to cast around for people to blame and to punish. How does this help? Surely it would be better to spend our time and energy on learning from the mistakes made and putting systems in place that will prevent such events from happening again.

> When we know there are people in difficulties or who find themselves in diminished circumstances, instead of spending effort on looking for people to blame, would it not be better to consider what difference needs to be made? To ask those in distress what support they really need and what are the ways that would help?

## Social care

Governments who have borrowed huge amounts to bail out banks, to stabilize economies, and prevent vital industries from closing down, have incurred enormous debts. It may take years, perhaps decades, to repay these debts.

The size of those repayments has required radical redistribution of national and local government funds. This is having, and will continue to have, an enormous impact on all government funded activities. Many social services are likely to be reduced in quantity and quality. Some might disappear altogether.

In most democratic nations much of the public purse is spent on activities that could fit under the banner of Social Care. This is a huge field that encompasses any activity that offers care and support to individuals and communities. The pinch of financial restraint is already being felt in most of these areas to the grave concern of those who are offering these services or who are in need of receipt of them. This situation is unlikely to improve for quite some time.

The quantity and quality of every type of social service are likely to be threatened by this situation. This is almost certain to result in dedicated workers losing their jobs and so will require increased effort from those remaining. In many areas, much of this social care is carried out through voluntary and community groups. Funding from government to support these groups is likely to be reduced or could be withdrawn altogether. Not only this, other funding agencies, philanthropic organizations and generous individuals, might find their resources reduced or could be called upon to spread them more thinly over a wider area.

There might be a temptation to rail against the injustice of this and perhaps to slide into a sense of despondency or despair. This is understandable, and yet, how does it help? Would it not be more beneficial to concentrate time, effort and energy on making a positive difference to as many of these areas as possible?

> If ever there was a time to shift from 'they' to 'we' surely that time is now!

## Part of the puzzle
Every one of us is a part of the puzzle that makes up our society.

> What a positive difference will be made when we all wake up to recognizing when we are each sometimes part of the problem and choosing instead to always be part of the solution!

Of course, many people have woken up to this already. Those are the people who are taking the following actions:

- ➤ Maintaining a realistically positive attitude and encouraging others to do the same.
- ➤ Finding small ways every day to be supportive to others.
- ➤ Volunteering their time and talents to help people who are less fortunate than themselves.
- ➤ Seeking out and joining with others who are intent upon making a positive difference to some aspect of their communities.
- ➤ Making simple everyday choices that contribute to environmental and social sustainability.

"We each make a difference in the world every moment through our words, actions and behavior, whether we are aware of it or not. The trick to being a smart human being is to choose to make a positive difference."

Choosing to be a regular or an occasional volunteer to help with or to improve some aspect of our world is a simple way to make that difference.

# MORE YOU MAKE THE DIFFERENCE BOOKS

Ripples created by our actions inevitably make some difference in the world. These books are intended to encourage and help people who want to make a positive difference to their lives and to the world around them.

## YOU MAKE THE DIFFERENCE
### through
## ENJOYABLE & EFFECTIVE MEETINGS

Following the guidelines for constructive participation, for efficient chairing and supportive facilitation, adopting the suggested attitudes, implementing the methods, skills, tools, essential procedures and useful processes will guarantee improved effectiveness and enjoyment of any meeting.

**YOU MAKE THE DIFFERENCE**
**Through**
**EFFORTLESS FACILITATION**

This book is packed with suggestions for planning and designing meetings and events, useful methods and tips for facilitation, empowering and productive processes and a variety of ready-made meeting designs to fit many situations. The implementation of these will guarantee inexperienced facilitators becoming skillful; and experienced facilitators becoming even more accomplished – effortlessly!

**YOU MAKE THE DIFFERENCE**
Through
**EMPOWERING VOLUNTEER MANAGMENT**

This book contains many suggestions for finding, recruiting, supporting, empowering, managing and keeping volunteers. Following these guidelines and using the insights into what volunteers need to be efficient, effective, valuable and fulfilled in their roles, will guarantee empowered volunteers.

## YOU MAKE THE DIFFERENCE
### Through
## SUCCESSFUL GROUPS & PROJECTS

This book offers insights into how groups work and why they sometimes fail, successful start-up and maintenance of projects that achieve the purpose and objectives, methods for attracting and keeping appropriate members and volunteers. The adoption and implementation of the suggested attitudes, the strategies for obtaining resources, the efficient use of time, money, skills and effort, and the respectful, cooperative ways people can enjoy working together will guarantee success of any group or project.

**YOU MAKE THE DIFFERENCE**
Through
**INSPIRING COMMUNITY**
**SUSTAINABILITY**

The answer to many of the difficulties facing society is creating a greater sense of community. This book is filled with information and insights, developed through decades of research and experience, on the elements essential for achieving sustainability in any form of community. Utilizing this information, adopting the suggested attitudes, and implementing the recommended systems and processes will guarantee greater sustainability in communities, whether they are rural or urban, traditional or intentional, Transition Towns or Ecovillages.

## YOU MAKE THE DIFFERENCE
### Through
## SMART TALKING

Each time we open our mouths to speak we will inevitably have an impact upon those to whom we are talking. This book aims to show the consequences of having a negative impact and offers insightful suggestions for creating a positive effect. Following these guidelines and the suggested attitudes, skills and tools that can relieve stress, enhance relationships and improve communication in so many areas of life will guarantee anyone becoming a Smart Talker.

**YOU MAKE THE DIFFERENCE**
Through
**SMART LISTENING**

Each of us will inevitably have an impact upon the individuals to whom we
listen that is either positive and beneficial or negative and potentially
damaging to individuals and society. Implementing the attitudes, listening
skills, tools and techniques suggested in this book will guarantee a positive
effect that will greatly improve personal and working relationships, reduce
conflict, enhance many areas of life and be supportive to people's
confidence and self-esteem.

**YOU MAKE THE DIFFERENCE**
Through
**SMART TALKING**
**& LISTENING TO CHILDREN**

From the moment children are born they are learning to become the adults who will manage the future. What kind of future might adults be influencing through the way they talk and listen to children? This book is crammed with skills, tools, insights and suggestions on how adults can be supportive through their communication to the development of youngsters and contribute towards a safe, sustainable future in the hands of well adjusted, capable, empowered, responsible and caring people.

# ABOUT
# YOU MAKE THE DIFFERENCE

Tim and Kay Kay, the two generations of cultural creatives who founded YOU MAKE THE DIFFERENCE, believe that it is now essential for people to behave supportively with one another, to become more engaged in their local community and to cooperate and work collaboratively for a sustainable future. The books and website are intended to encourage and support people to achieve the positive difference they wish to make in their lives and in the world around them.

To help with this, Kay Kay, the author, offers decades of experience gained in a variety of professions and cultures, and shares her practical philosophy, knowledge, skills and insights into beneficial ways of behaving, working and communicating with one another and contributing to society.

Tim, as collaborator, book designer, publisher and Webmaster, brings his creativity as an artist and writer, his in-depth knowledge of Buddhist philosophy and the skills and considerable experience gained through living, working and studying in many countries.

All the YOU MAKE THE DIFFERENCE books are intended to be enjoyable to read and easy to use - by everyone. The wealth of information is concisely written to be of benefit to professionals wishing to upgrade their skills; busy people working to make a difference in their communities and at the grassroots of their societies, and people from different cultures, especially those from the developing world, for whom English may be a 2nd or even 3rd language.

On the website: www.youmakethedifference.net there is more background information; GUIDES on a variety of interesting and useful subjects that are FREE to download, and the opportunity for people to become part of the Global YOU MAKE THE DIFFERENCE network.

*"We each make a difference in the world every moment through our words, actions and behavior, whether we are aware of it or not. The trick to being a smart human being is to choose to make a positive difference."*

Kay Kay